Pests and diseases

Pests and diseases

Andrew Halstead
and Béatrice Henricot

DK

LONDON, NEW YORK, MUNICH, MELBOURNE, DELHI

PROJECT EDITOR Emma Callery
PROJECT ART EDITOR Alison Shackleton
SENIOR EDITOR Helen Fewster
MANAGING EDITOR Esther Ripley
MANAGING ART EDITOR Alison Donovan
PICTURE RESEARCH Ria Jones, Frances Vargo
PRODUCTION EDITORS Kavita Varma, Tony Phipps

US CONSULTANT Delilah Smittle
US EDITOR Christine Heilman

First American Edition, 2010
DK Publishing
375 Hudson Street, New York, New York 10014

2 4 6 8 10 9 7 5 3 1

[176598—March 2010]

Published in Great Britain by Dorling Kindersley Limited.

A catalog record for this book is available from the
Library of Congress.

ISBN 978-0-7566-5910-3

Printed and bound by Star Standard Pte Ltd, Singapore

DK books are available at special discounts when
purchased in bulk for sales promotions, premiums,
fund-raising, or educational use. For details, contact:
DK Publishing Special Markets, 375 Hudson Street,
New York, New York 10014 or SpecialSales@dk.com.

Discover more at
www.dk.com

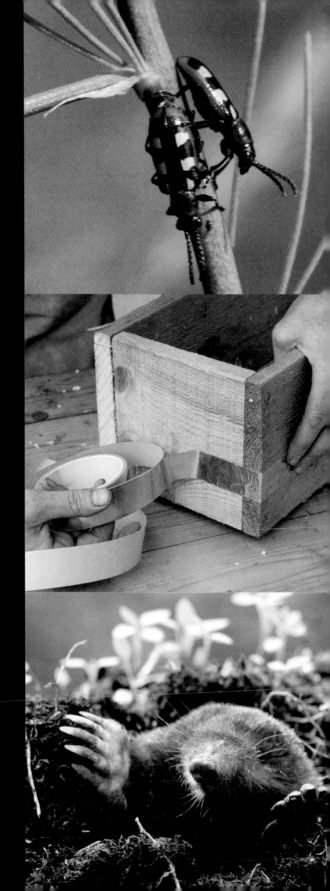

Contents

Andrew Halstead and Béatrice Henricot
Andrew Halstead is the Royal Horticultural
Society's Principal Entomologist and Béatrice
Henricot is Principal Pathologist. They both have
many years of experience of identifying and
dealing with garden pests and diseases.

Healthy gardening

The healthy growth of plants can be affected by pests and diseases, nutrient deficiencies, and disorders caused by environmental stresses. It is generally the case that if you grow your plants well, they are less likely to succumb to pests and diseases. Selecting resistant varieties or generally vigorous plants will help prevent problems. Also choose suitable plants for the soil and position of your garden, and give them plenty of water, otherwise they may be permanently damaged or even killed. Good gardening practices help prevent pests and diseases from taking hold.

The benefits of healthy gardening

Growing a wide range of plants can reduce the impact of pests and diseases. Some plants may suffer damage but others are spared. Where large numbers of a few plants are grown, it is easier for pests and diseases to cause serious harm.

Pictures clockwise from far left

Fruit trees Long-lived plants, such as fruit trees and bushes, can build up pest and disease problems over the years. Aphids, mildews, and virus diseases are potential problems to watch for. Put up a bluebird nest box—bluebirds will collect hundreds of insects a day while they are rearing their chicks.

Flower borders Flower beds planted with annuals, bulbs, and herbaceous plants provide interest through much of the year. Plants in flower from spring to fall support butterflies and bees, providing them with nectar and pollen. Bees are essential pollinating insects for many fruits and other plants.

Vegetable gardens Growing some ornamental plants, such as African or French marigolds, close to vegetables will attract hoverflies and other aphid predators, which will help to control aphids on beans and other susceptible plants. Crop rotation helps to avoid the buildup of some vegetable pests and diseases, especially those that are soilborne.

Garden ponds Pond plants have few significant pests or diseases. The presence of water adds a valuable habitat for frogs and toads, which help control slugs and insect pests.

Long grass Most grass in gardens is maintained as mown lawn, but some can be left uncut as an informal meadow or prairie area. Native wildflowers can be grown to encourage insects, birds, and other wildlife by providing shelter and food in the form of nectar, pollen, and seeds.

Right plant, right place

Plants differ in the conditions they require for optimum growth. Before planting a garden, consider factors such as soil type, drainage, whether it has a sunny or shaded exposure, and how cold the winters will be. Plants that prefer or at least tolerate local conditions are more likely to thrive and will be more tolerant of pests and diseases.

Pictures clockwise from right

Sunny gardens Sunny conditions suit the majority of garden plants, giving gardeners a wide choice of fruits, vegetables, and ornamental plants that can be grown. Sunny gardens can also be dry gardens, especially in sandy and other free-draining soils. In such situations, it is wise to select drought-tolerant plants to avoid the need for frequent watering. A mulch of rotted compost or other organic material on the soil surface helps retain soil moisture throughout the year.

Shaded gardens Shade can be provided by buildings, tall fences, walls, hedges, or trees. With trees and hedges, there is the added problem of these larger plants taking most of the available moisture and nutrients from the soil. Plants that need good light are likely to grow in a spindly fashion in heavy shade. The plants best suited for these conditions are spring bulbs, ferns, and ornamental plants that naturally grow in woodland situations.

Acidic and alkaline soils Some plants, such as heathers, rhododendrons, azaleas, and camellias, need acidic soil with a pH value of less than 7 (*see p.14*). If grown in an alkaline soil, where the pH value will be 7 or more, the foliage becomes yellow and the plants are likely to die. While most plants can be grown in acidic soil, the choice for alkaline soils is more restricted.

Coastal gardens Gardens close to coastlines are frequently windswept, and plants can be damaged by salt spray. It is often necessary to plant a shelter belt of wind-tolerant trees or shrubs in order to provide more favorable conditions for the rest of the yard. Coastal gardens tend to enjoy a much milder climate than those inland, which means that less hardy plants can be grown successfully outdoors.

Choosing your plants

When it comes to susceptibility to pests and diseases, not all plants are equal. Well grown and vigorous plants are less likely to suffer problems. Some cultivars have been bred to be resistant or more tolerant of certain pests and diseases.

Pictures clockwise from left

Resistant plants Roses suffer from several debilitating fungal diseases, such as mildew, black spot, and rust. These diseases require regular treatment with fungicides throughout the growing season. Fortunately, some roses have been bred that are resistant to or relatively unaffected by these diseases. Other resistant fruits, vegetables, and ornamental plants are available, and it is worth looking for such cultivars in seed and nursery catalogs.

Specialty nurseries Plants obtained from a specialty nursery may be more expensive than those from a home improvement store's garden section, but they are often of better quality. The grower is also likely to be able to supply expert knowledge on the best ways to grow and care for the plants.

AAS plants All-America Selections Winners are flowers and vegetables that are considered to be excellent cultivars for garden cultivation. Winners are chosen by a network of independent judges for their superior performance in North American gardens. Factors taken into consideration include weather and disease resistance, vigorous growth, yield, attractiveness, and flavor for edibles. By choosing AAS Winners, you will improve the quality of plants in your garden and avoid some of the inferior cultivars that are available.

Choose healthy plants Look carefully at plants before you buy them. Select those with a healthy appearance and a good growth habit. Avoid plants with yellowing or wilted foliage, or those that have grown too tall for their pots. A dense growth of moss or weeds on the soil surface tells you the plant has been on the sale bench for a long time. Pick bulbs and corms that are large, firm, and without signs of decay or dryness. Look for signs of pests or diseases and don't take them home with you!

Understanding the nutrients in your soil

Good soil provides water, air, and nutrients for healthy plant growth. All soils are not ideal for every kind of cultivation, but all can be improved. To choose plants that are suited to your soil characteristics, first you need to recognize your soil type.

What is soil? Soil is formed from the breakdown of rocks into particles of sand, silt, and clay. These particles make up half the soil volume; the rest is air, water, living organisms, and humus. Types of garden soils can be defined by the proportion of sand, silt, and clay particles they contain and their pH. The ideal soil for gardeners is loam, which contains sand, silt, and clay in relatively even proportions. Soil is the source of plant mineral nutrients. Those required in high quantities are nitrogen, phosphorus, and potassium (N-P-K). Other important nutrients, such as calcium, sulfur, iron, and boron, are required in small quantities. The nutrient content of any soil can be improved using fertilizers (*see p.19*).

pH test

A pH test is a means of chemically testing the acidity or alkalinity of a soil. Very generally, acidic soil has a pH value below 7.7 is considered neutral, and above 7, the soil is alkaline. Soil pH influences the availability of nutrients to plants. Many ornamental plants grow best in soil at about pH 7; for most vegetables, a pH 6–6.5 is suitable (brassicas prefer a pH 7.5). Lime-hating plants, such as heather, rhododendrons, and camellias, prefer a pH 5.1–6.

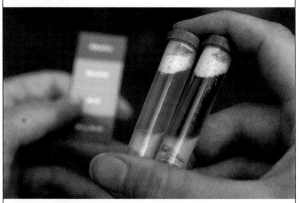

Chemical soil kits available in many garden centers are easy to use to check the pH values of the soil in the garden.

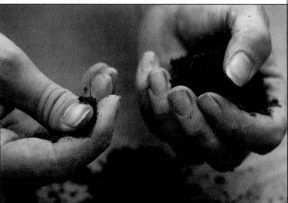

Sandy soil Sandy soil has large particles surrounded by air spaces. It tends to be gritty and fall apart in your hand when rolled into a ball. It is easy to cultivate and warms up quickly in the spring, but it dries out fast, and minerals and nutrients are leached easily. Acidification can occur rapidly as the calcium is washed out easily. Adding organic matter (*see p.16*) improves water retention, fertility, and structure. Mulching reduces evaporation and erosion.

Clay soil Clay soil tends to be sticky when wet. Take a handful of moist topsoil and squeeze it into a ball; if it keeps its shape, it has a high clay content. It is reluctant to dry, but when it does, it can set hard, shrink, and crack. In general, clay soil has good nutrient concentrations, but it can become waterlogged, resulting in root problems. Clay soil benefits from organic matter. Nonorganic material, such as horticultural grit and perlite, helps its structure.

The effects of nutrient deficiency

Nitrogen deficiency causes leaves to be small and chlorotic; they may turn yellow or red, and growth is reduced. It is more common in heavily cropped soil or one with low organic content. Unrotted organic matter, such as wood chips, may deprive the soil of nitrogen.

Phosphorus deficiency causes reduction in flowering and fruiting, and, in general, poor plant growth. The leaves develop a purplish discoloration, are small, and fall early. Phosphorus deficiency is most commonly seen on acidic soil or following heavy rain or watering.

Potassium deficiency causes leaf scorching and curling. Flowers and fruit may be reduced. Plants that require a lot of potassium, such as tomatoes (deficiency causes blotchy ripening), beans, and fruits, are more likely to suffer. It is more common on sandy or peaty soil.

Calcium deficiency is often seen on acidic soil or any inadequately watered soil, which stops the plant from taking up calcium. Commonly, it causes blossom end rot of tomatoes (a black patch at the fruit's flower end) and bitter pit of apples (dark spots appear under the skin).

Iron deficiency causes yellowing between the leaf veins and is more apparent on young leaves. In severe cases, leaves look white and scorching of the margins and tips occur. Often seen with manganese deficiency, it commonly occurs when acid-loving plants are grown in alkaline soil.

Magnesium deficiency causes the older leaves to yellow between the veins, sometimes with brown areas (necrosis). In severe cases, leaves may wither and fall, leading to crop loss. It is typically seen on sandy soil during wet periods. Magnesium is made unavailable by excess potassium.

Caring for your soil

There is a variety of soil improvers to amend difficult soil. Fertilizers provide a concentrated supply of one or more plant nutrients, but they have little impact on the soil structure. Soil conditioners, like farmyard manure and garden compost, have low fertilizer value, but they condition the soil.

Digging in organic matter

Animal manures are useful for heavy and light soils alike. They need to be composted for at least a year, as they release ammonia, which can scorch young or tender plants. Dig them into the soil in the fall.

Plant waste, such as garden compost and composted bark, improves soil texture and contributes to fertility. Apply as with manures. Spent mushroom compost is a good soil conditioner but not around lime-hating plants due to its lime content. Leafmold is excellent for structurally improving soils, but low in nutritional value.

Plants grown as manure crops (green manures) are good options for fallow areas. They provide ground cover to smother weeds and to store soil nutrients, preventing leaching during non-crop periods. When the land is needed, dig the green manure plant back in so it rots down, releasing nutrients and adding organic matter.

Mulching

Mulches are a loose covering of biodegradable or nonbiodegradable materials. They suppress weeds, improve moisture retention, and regulate soil temperature.

Biodegradable mulches, such as compost, manure, leafmold, and bark, play the most important role in soil management. They add organic matter to the soil, unlike nonbiodegradable mulches, such as plastic sheeting, gravel, or glass chips.

All organic mulches decompose completely in the soil due to the activities of soilborne organisms, such as worms and saprophytic fungi. As a result, the structure of the soil and the nutrient availability is improved.

Before applying mulch, it is essential that the soil is wet and warm. The mulch should be spread evenly. Soil structure can be improved with a layer as thin as ½ in (1 cm), but to control weeds effectively, a 3–4-in (8–10-cm) layer of mulch is needed. Keep mulch away from the stems of woody plants.

Composting

Composting is a biochemical process in which organic matter is decomposed by naturally occurring organisms to produce a stable, soil-like end product called compost. It provides a means of converting waste materials from both the kitchen and the yard into a free, environmentally friendly source of organic matter, which can be used to improve soil fertility, conserve soil moisture, and enhance plant growth. It also helps the community as a whole by reducing landfill use.

The microorganisms involved in the composting process need air, moisture, and nitrogen to efficiently decompose the organic matter. This is why air should be allowed in from the sides and base of the compost pile. If the pile shows signs of drying out, apply water. Moisture can be retained by covering the pile with burlap, old carpet, or plastic sheeting.

A compost pile is ideally placed in a sheltered and shady area. There are many types of homemade and commercial compost bins. They should be around 4 ft (1.2 m) tall for good results, but can be much wider than tall. Once the material has a dark, crumbly texture, it is ready to use. The transformation can take from three months to two years, depending on the temperature of the pile.

Add kitchen waste Kitchen and garden waste makes good compost if properly mixed, but do not let one particular component take over. Ideally, make the compost a mix of one-third soft, green, and sappy material (grass clippings, raw vegetable peelings, tea leaves) and two-thirds hard brown materials (twigs, straw, newspapers).

Composting worms Unlike most earthworms, these are striped and live in decaying organic matter. At least 100 worms are needed to start a worm compost bin. They are more productive at 64–77°F (18–25°C) in compost that is moist but not wet. The bins should have a large surface area and be rainproof, insulated, and well ventilated.

Good garden hygiene

Healthy plants are more able to fight off pests and diseases. Recently planted or propagated plants are most vulnerable, so take extra care to protect them.

Raking leaves It is best to rake leaves in the fall and use them to make leafmold (but make sure you burn any infected plant material). Leaves left lying on the ground will create a microclimate favorable to some fungal infections, or harbor pests and diseases.

Caring for your plants

Good hygiene is important to avoid a buildup of pests and diseases in the garden. Soaking pots in a mild bleach solution followed by a water rinse helps avoid fungal infections. To ensure healthy growth, sow seeds at the appropriate time and always give new plants plenty of water, which is the most common cause of failure of newly established plants. Wiping tools after pruning plants is a good practice, too. If the plants are diseased, clean tools even more frequently. Many diseases and pests overwinter on fallen material, so their removal after the growing season gives your plants a better chance to grow healthily in the spring.

Sterilizing Using cutting tools on an infected plant and then on a healthy one without disinfecting them can spread disease. Similarly, pots, trays, and work surfaces should be cleaned with disinfectant to minimize the spread of pests and diseases.

Feeding This is usually done when plants grow rapidly during the spring and early summer. Organic fertilizers provide a variety of nutrients, while inorganic or synthetic fertilizers can be general-purpose, containing equal quantities of N-P-K, or single-nutrient compounds.

Watering This is important during the critical stages of a plant's development, such as seedlings and when flowers and fruits are being produced. Water in the evening to minimize soil evaporation, and water at the base of plants, not on the foliage, to reduce risk of foliar diseases.

Weeding Weeds will outcompete the plants we want to grow as ornamentals and crops by depriving them of nutrients, water, and light. They are also reservoirs for some pests and diseases (such as viruses). Aim to remove weeds before they produce seeds.

Pruning for health

Poor pruning can increase the likelihood of infection from disease and, to some extent, pests. Equally, some types of pruning are carried out only for the purpose of removing diseased or infested plant material.

Why prune?

Pruning is carried out to restrict a plant to a specified size and shape, to remove excess branches that are rubbing together, and to remove broken, damaged, or diseased branches or double leaders. Pruning also gives the opportunity to remove very thin or crossing shoots from the center. This will open up the center of the plant and allow more light and air to flow through the crown.

Most homeowners should limit tree pruning to small branches that can be reached from the ground. For large branches, hire professional tree experts with proper equipment and insurance.

Remove dead/diseased wood If the branches are dying from a stem infection, such as nectria canker or silver leaf, the infection may be removed if the diseased wood is cut out promptly. This also reduces the inoculum available to initiate new infections.

Crossing and rubbing branches Branches that cross or rub damage the bark, creating entry points for pathogens such as wood decay fungi. Prune out these branches and apply a wound sealant if wounding occurs during the dormant season.

Thin dense growth Improving air ventilation in this way reduces the chance of infection of many airborne fungi. Reduce the older stems of flowering shrubs by one-third every year to stimulate the production of new shoots and create a microclimate less favorable to infection.

Correct cuts

Remove branches correctly by cutting them with clean, sharp tools, since rough cuts or torn branches can promote disease development. Also use good quality pruners to prune stems up to pencil-size thickness, but use then use loppers or pruning saws for anything larger. Loppers and pruning saws are designed to cut through wood smoothly and cleanly. Pole pruners with telescopic handles can be used for high branches from the ground and chain saws can be used on the largest of branches, but are not recommended for use by the home owner. You must always wear gloves when pruning, and burn diseased material.

Make sure that you cut branches at a slant next to a bud that can produce new growth, and do not make cuts flush with the trunk.

In the past, part of the standard recommendation for pruning trees was to apply a wound paint to all fresh cuts. This treatment is now less in favor, as it is believed to interfere with the healing process. However, the treatment might still be useful to protect wounds that occur in the dormant season.

Remove branches correctly Do not cut off branches absolutely flush with the stem, as this will impair the growth of the scar tissue. It is best to make the cut just outside the swollen area at the base of the branch (called the branch collar) that sometimes has a bark ridge.

Cut out unhealthy branches These cuts are usually best carried out as soon as the symptoms are seen rather than waiting for the appropriate pruning time. Make the cut well below the infected tissue, which can be recognized by staining below the bark.

Prune above an outward-facing bud Always prune above a strong bud or healthy side shoot to create an open, uncongested center. The cut should slope away from the bud or shoot. Pruning too close to a bud will cause damage and too far away will result in dieback.

Vegetable gardens

Rotating groups of vegetables on a three- or four-year plan is a simple procedure that prevents the buildup of pests and diseases without the use of chemicals.

Companion planting Growing one type of plant can be beneficial to another plant growing in the vicinity. For example, yellow- or orange-flowered plants attract insects which, in turn, can prey on pests that are feeding on crops growing nearby.

Three-year crop rotation

The most common rotation is the three-year plan. Divide the vegetable garden into three sections, and each year grow a different crop in each section, giving a two-year gap between each group of crops.

Crops are usually grouped into peas and beans, brassicas, and root vegetables, as each of these groups have similar cultivation requirements. It also gives a chance for pests and diseases that are specific to a group of crops to die away. Crop rotation is of limited use for pathogens and pests that have a very broad host range and also for those that can survive for a very long time in the soil. If you have enough room, consider a four-year plan where potatoes are planted as a fourth crop.

Strict rotation might be impractical in small areas; if this is the case, grow plants wherever it is convenient. If any problems arise, it is best to choose a new place for planting, or grow in containers with sterile potting mix.

Year 1
The pea family includes peas, green beans, broad beans (fava beans), and green manures, such as vetches and alfalfa. They require organic matter but little fertilizer. Their roots can fix nitrogen, which helps crops the following year. After harvest, cut down plants and leave roots to rot. Rotation helps to prevent diseases such as fusarium wilt and downy mildews and pests such as pea thrips.

Year 2
The brassica family includes Brussels sprouts, broccoli, cabbages, cauliflower, rutabagas, turnips, and radishes. Brassicas need fertile soil and should follow plants from the pea family. They benefit from alkaline soil, so check the pH (see p.14) and lime the soil if the pH is too low. Rotation will prevent diseases such as ring spot, white rust, downy mildews, and, to some extent, clubroot.

Year 3
Root crops include carrots, parsley, parsnips, and salsify, which need moderate fertilization. Rotation helps prevent diseases such as parsnip canker. Or plant tomatoes and potatoes in year three. They need lots of fertilizers and organic matter. Planting potatoes ensures that the soil is well cultivated. Rotation reduces potato cyst nematodes, potato spraing, and powdery scab.

What are pests and diseases?

Garden plants are continually exposed to fungi, bacteria, viruses, insects, and many other creatures that have the potential to cause damage. Fortunately, a plant's natural defenses are able to resist most attacks and the environment is not always favorable for them to occur in the first place. Recognizing symptoms and their distribution on the plant is very important in identifying the cause of the problem. Once that is known, it is much easier to see how to overcome the pest or disease.

Know your enemy: pests

Pests large and small occur in all gardens, and most plants will at some time be affected by them. Knowing what the problems are likely to be will help prevent serious damage.

Parsleyworm caterpillar Parsleyworm caterpillar is the larva of the beautiful black swallowtail butterfly. It feeds on foliage of the parsley family, including celery, dill, and carrots. Grow healthy plants to withstand light damage, and encourage birds to keep the caterpillars in check.

All parts of plants can be attacked by pests, from the roots to the shoot tips. Some pests are of microscopic size, such as nematodes or eelworms and some mites. Their identification therefore often depends on recognizing the symptoms they cause on the plants. Other pests, such as birds and mammals, are easily seen. In between is a large array of smaller pests, such as insects, mites, woodlice, millipedes, slugs, and snails. Most are visible to the naked eye, but a magnifying glass is sometimes needed to see the smaller pests more clearly.

Pests damage plants in various ways. Insects, such as beetles, moth and butterfly caterpillars, sawflies, and earwigs, have biting mouthparts that they use to eat holes in foliage, flowers, fruits, and roots. Other insects, such as aphids, whitefly, mealybugs, scales, thrips, plant bugs, and mites, have sucking mouthparts that they insert into plant tissues in order to feed on sap. Some insects, mites, and nematodes cause plants to produce abnormal growths known as galls, in which the gall-formers live and feed.

While most pests attack plants from the outside, there are some that feed internally, such as leaf miners, stem borers, and fruit pests—codling moth caterpillars, for example (*see p.122*).

Mammals and birds Squirrels, deer, rabbits, rats, and mice can cause serious damage to plants, as can pigeons and other pest birds. Other mammals, such as cats, dogs and foxes, do not necessarily eat garden plants but can be a nuisance (*see pp.35–37*).

Above-ground pests Caterpillars, sawfly larvae, beetles, earwigs, leaf miners, aphids, scale insects, leafhoppers, mealybugs, plant bugs, and thrips are examples of pests that feed on foliage, stems, flowers, and fruits. For more information, see pages 30–32.

Soil pests Cutworms, chafer grubs, vine weevil larvae (illustrated), leatherjackets, carrot fly, cabbage root fly, wireworms, and root aphids are all pests that live in the soil and feed on roots. Small plants may be killed or have their growth checked (*see pp.33 and 34*).

Pest life cycles

Most pests start life as an egg, although some, such as aphids, give birth to live young. Between the egg and the adult stage, there is a period during which the immature nymphs or larvae feed and increase in size before finally becoming adults capable of reproduction, and then the cycle begins again.

Metamorphosis

Invertebrate animals can make the transition from egg to adult by two different processes. Some, such as slugs, snails, woodlice, earwigs, suckers, scale insects, mealybugs, whiteflies, aphids, thrips, and mites, undergo incomplete metamorphosis. The immature stages are not greatly different from the adult, except in size and lack of wings for the insects.

Complete metamorphosis occurs in butterflies and moths, beetles, flies, sawflies, and ants. Here the immature feeding stage is a caterpillar, grub, or maggot that is very different from the adult insect. When the larva has completed its feeding, it goes into a stage known as a pupa or chrysalis. During the pupal stage, the larval tissues break down and are reconstructed to form the adult insect.

The cabbage white butterfly is an insect that goes through complete metamorphosis, going from an egg to a caterpillar to a pupa or chrysalis before emerging as an adult butterfly. As with many pests with this life cycle, it is the caterpillar or larval stage that causes the damage.

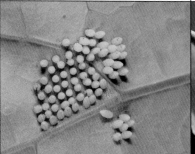

Cabbage white eggs
Batches of pale yellow eggs are laid on the underside of cabbage and other brassica leaves, with two generations occurring during the summer months.

Cabbage white caterpillar
The eggs hatch into yellow and black caterpillars that devour the leaves of their host plants. The caterpillars shed their outer skin five times as they grow larger.

Cabbage white pupa
When the caterpillar has completed its feeding, it crawls away to find a vertical surface that it can attach itself to and subsequently change into a chrysalis or pupa.

Surviving the winter

Pests can remain active throughout the year in greenhouses or on houseplants, but most invertebrate garden pests go into a resting or dormant stage as temperatures fall and days get shorter in the fall. They may overwinter as eggs, as immature nymphs and larvae, as pupae, or as adults. Those pests that overwinter as immature nymphs, larvae, or adults generally seek sheltered places in which to do so, such as in the soil, underneath loose bark, or in dense shrubby growth, such as conifer hedges.

In the spring, warmer weather brings plants back into growth and encourages pests out of their dormant phase. The hatching of aphid eggs on fruit trees and bushes, for example, is closely coordinated with the emergence of foliage from the buds. Both the eggs and the buds are responding to the same environmental conditions.

Earwig with eggs Earwigs overwinter as adult insects in the soil. The females lay their eggs in midwinter and remain with them until they hatch. The earwig is one of the few insects that show parental care for their eggs and young nymphs.

When pests thrive

Light infestations of pests have little impact, but as their numbers increase, the feeding pressure on garden plants becomes increasingly obvious. Plant growth may slow down, particularly where pests are feeding at the shoot tips and distorting the new growth. The foliage also becomes marked by holes where caterpillars and other pests have eaten parts of the leaves. Damage in late summer is of less significance because by then the growing season is coming to an end and so the consequences for the plant are less.

Population explosions

Small pests often have rapid reproductive rates that allow heavy infestations to develop quickly. Most pests are helped by warm conditions and develop much more rapidly when temperatures are high. This may allow them to produce several generations during the summer. Predators, parasites, and diseases can keep pests at a low level, but if these natural controls are not operating, pests can breed unchecked. Sometimes the use of pesticides does more harm than good by eliminating the pest's natural enemies, giving the pest a free run.

Snails and slugs Most pests like it warm and dry, but snails and slugs prefer cool damp conditions, which is why they do most of their feeding at night or after rain. These pests are particularly damaging to seedlings and soft young growth on herbaceous plants—for information on traps, see page 56.

Aphid outbreaks Greenfly and blackfly reproduce rapidly throughout the spring and summer months. The all-female populations of these pests shorten the life cycle by giving birth to live young instead of laying eggs. This can result in plants becoming heavily infested in just a few weeks.

Above-ground pests

Pests that feed above ground are easier to detect than those that live in the soil, and the damage they cause is also more obvious. All above-ground parts of plants, including the stem, foliage, flowers, and fruits or seeds, can be damaged by pests—and in many different ways, as shown here.

Some pests suck sap, which can result in stunted growth or distorted leaves. Other pests eat holes in the foliage and flowers, while yet others are internal feeders that tunnel through the stems, leaves, or fruits.

There are various other ways that pests can damage plants. For example, sap-sucking insects, such as some aphids, leafhoppers, and thrips, can spread plant virus diseases (see p.41) on their mouthparts when they move from plant to plant.

In addition, aphids, whitefly, mealybugs, and some scale insects excrete a sugary substance, called honeydew, which makes the foliage sticky. Black sooty molds then often develop on the honeydew, causing further disfigurement to the plant. Other pests, particularly some insects and mites, induce abnormal growths known as galls (see p.68).

Ants
These familiar insects nest in the soil, but they climb plants to visit aphids to collect the sweet honeydew they excrete. Ants cause little direct damage to plants, but they can be a nuisance and they protect aphids by driving ladybugs away.

Beetles
There are many beetle pests. Japanese beetle is a serious foliage and flower pest of roses, hibiscus, grapes, hostas, and other plants. Lily leaf beetle (p.100), asparagus beetle (p.121), and viburnum beetle (p.81) eat foliage in both the adult and grub stages.

Caterpillars
Caterpillars are the larval stage of butterflies and moths. Most species are not pests, but some have caterpillars that most distinctly are, eating holes in leaves, boring into stems and fruits, or eating roots. Some of the smallest caterpillars feed within the leaves as leaf miners. Caterpillars can be distinguished from similar larvae of sawflies (see overleaf) by counting the clasping legs on the abdomen. Sawfly larvae have at least seven pairs, whereas butterfly and moth caterpillars have five or fewer. Control methods are given on pages 50–63; for specific hosts see pages 64–139.

Aphids

Also known as greenfly, blackfly, and plant lice, aphids suck sap from most garden plants using their needlelike mouthparts. Heavy infestations stunt growth and soil the plant with their sticky excrement (honeydew) and resulting sooty mold. For most of the spring and summer, aphids are wingless females that give birth to live young. When the aphids need to move on to another host plant, winged forms of the aphid develop. Many overwinter as eggs laid in the fall on the branches of trees and shrubs. Control methods are given for specific hosts on pages 64–139.

Earwigs

Earwigs hide in dark places during the day. At night they emerge to eat soft foliage and the petals of flowers, such as dahlia, chrysanthemum, and clematis (see p.84). In some years earwigs can be particularly abundant and damaging.

Spittlebug

This frothy white liquid is often seen in early summer on lavender (see p.131) and many other plants. It is secreted by a creamy-white froghopper nymph that is sucking sap from the stems. Despite the spit's obvious presence, little real damage is caused to the plants.

Plant bugs

These sap-sucking insects attack the shoot tips, flowers, buds, and fruits, especially apples (see p.122), killing cells in the developing leaves and blooms. As a result, the expanding leaves tear, forming many small holes, and flower buds shrivel or open unevenly.

Leafcutter bees

The females cut pieces of leaf from the edges of roses and other plants. These are flown to the nest tunnel in dry soil, rotten wood, or a hollow plant stem and used to form cells in which larvae develop. The adult bees are pollinators so are best tolerated.

Above-ground pests *continued*

Moths

Moths mainly fly at night, when they lay eggs on their host plants. It is the caterpillar stage that does the damage (*see p.30*). Some moth larvae are leaf miners. Control methods are given on pages 50–63 and for specific hosts see pages 64–139.

Wasps

Wasps can inflict painful stings and cause damage to ripening fruits. These social insects live in communal nests that are headed by a queen wasp with several hundred worker wasps. Adult wasps eat other insects, some of which may be garden pests.

Sawflies

Sawflies have caterpillar-like larvae with seven or more pairs of clasping legs on their abdomens. Sawfly larvae often feed together in groups and can quickly devour the foliage of certain trees, shrubs, and herbaceous plants. When disturbed, they grip the leaf with the legs on their thorax and wave their abdomens, giving an S-shape to their bodies. Other sawfly pests feed as larvae inside developing fruits or as leaf miners. Adult sawflies do not damage plants. Control methods are given for specific hosts on pages 64–139.

Scale insects

Scales are sap-sucking insects that infest the stems and foliage of many plants. Some produce a sugary excrement, known as honeydew, that makes plants sticky and allows the growth of sooty molds. The soft-bodied insects are covered by shells or scales. When mature, some scale insects deposit their eggs beneath their shells, but others, such as cushion scales, secrete a white, waxy material in which the eggs are embedded. These egg masses are often more visible than the scale itself. Control methods are given for specific hosts on pages 64–139.

Leaf miners

Most leaf miners are fly or moth larvae, but there are some leaf-mining sawflies and beetles. They make distinctive discolored lines or blotches in the foliage where they have been eating the tissues. Control methods are given for specific hosts on pages 64–139.

Virus vectors

It is mainly sap-sucking insects that transmit virus diseases when they move from one plant to another. Aphids, leafhoppers, and thrips are often responsible, but some soil-dwelling nematodes also spread virus diseases, especially on soft fruit.

Soil- and root-dwelling pests

Soil-dwelling pests are mostly hidden from view but can have a severe effect on plants because a healthy root system is essential for good growth.

Soil pests range in size from microscopic nematodes or eelworms to insects, millipedes, woodlice, and slugs that can be readily seen with the naked eye. If a large proportion of the root system is damaged, plants can be killed, especially if the damage occurs when the plant is still at an early stage of its growth. Root vegetables, such as carrots and turnips, can survive attacks by root fly larvae, but the plants are made unfit for human consumption by the damage.

Some creatures found in the soil, such as millipedes and woodlice, feed mainly on decaying plant material. They may nibble seedlings but they are unlikely to harm established plants.

Soil-dwelling pests are often difficult to control because of their hidden nature and a lack of suitable pesticides for use in this situation.

Root aphids
Root aphids live underground and suck sap from the roots and the base of stems on plants such as lettuce, beans, carrots, auricula (pictured), and other ornamental plants. Infested plants lack vigor and tend to wilt in sunny weather. Control is difficult; on edible plants, crop rotation (*see p.23*) may help.

Wireworms
Wireworms grow up to 1 in (25 mm) long and have rather stiff, yellowish-orange bodies. They are the larval stage of click beetles, but only the larval stage causes damage. They can kill seedling plants and bore into potato tubers, root vegetables, and onion bulbs. Large numbers of wireworms live in grasslands, where they cause no noticeable damage. However, the first year or two of cultivation on a newly dug plot can see heavy damage to vegetables growing on the site. There is no insecticide available for their control in gardens.

Vine weevil grubs
The creamy white, legless grubs of vine weevils are mainly a problem on plants grown in pots or other containers, but also occur in open ground. They are fully grown as larvae in fall to spring, which is when plants can be killed. Control methods are on page 138.

Chafer grubs
Larger than vine weevil grubs, these pests have three pairs of legs at the head end, curved bodies. and as adults are beetles. They eat grass roots and can kill small ornamental plants and vegetables. Control methods are given on page 104.

Invertebrate pests

Invertebrate pests are small creatures without backbones, such as nematodes or eelworms, slugs and snails, insects, mites, millipedes, and woodlice. Many are not garden pests, but a minority can cause problems.

Gardens and greenhouses are home to a wide range of invertebrate animals. Some are welcome as pollinators, predators, and parasites of pests, or as recyclers of dead plant materials. Many others live and feed in gardens without being either beneficial to gardeners or causing problems through damaging plants. The minority that are pests soon make their presence felt by the adverse effects they have on plant growth and appearance.

All parts of plants are potentially at risk from these predators. Most of the damage is seen on the foliage and flowers, but there are unseen pests that feed on roots or inside the stems and fruits of plants.

Some examples of different types of the invertebrate animals that are more commonly found in gardens are shown on this page.

Slugs and snails
Snails differ from slugs in having a shell into which they can withdraw their bodies. Both types of mollusks secrete a slimy substance from their bodies, and this can leave a silvery trail where they have moved over a plant. They feed by rasping the surface of leaves, stems, and flowers with their "tongues," Nonchemical treatments for slugs and snails are given on pages 56, 58–59, and 63, and see also using pellets on page 53.

Mites
Most mites have four pairs of legs as adults. Gall mites have only two pairs. Some, such as gall mites, induce abnormal growths. Control methods are given for specific hosts on pages 64–139.

Woodlice
Woodlice are terrestrial crustaceans that hide during the day in dark, damp places. They feed at night, mainly on decaying plant material, but can damage seedlings or enlarge damage started by other pests.

Millipedes
Millipedes are often found with woodlice and have similar feeding habits. They have elongate segmented bodies, with two pairs of legs on each segment. There is no insecticidal control for these invertebrates.

Insects
Adult insects have segmented bodies with three pairs of legs and, in most species, two pairs of wings on the thorax. They include beetles, flies, moths, sawflies, thrips, aphids, and whitefly.

Mammals and birds

Birds and mammals are less abundant than the smaller garden pests, but they have bigger appetites and some can be a nuisance in the garden, even if they are not eating the plants.

Birds and mammals can be some of the most difficult problems that gardeners have to contend with. In most cases, it is not possible or advisable to kill these animals, even where it is legal to do so. Netting or fencing can be effective in protecting plants (*see pp.58–59*) from some of these pests, but it can be expensive and may detract from the appearance of your garden.

Various repellent substances and scaring devices are available (*see also pp.58–59*), but they generally do not give effective long-term protection. Repellent substances rely on an unpleasant smell or taste; frequent applications are often needed to maintain protection. Scaring devices range from scarecrows to devices that emit ultrasonic sound. These can be effective when newly installed, but birds and mammals get used to them after a while. With problem birds and mammals, it is a matter of trying to limit the damage caused.

Foxes
Increasingly common in urban areas, foxes damage lawns in search of chafer grubs (*see p.33*) and foul gardens with their feces and strong-smelling urine. They will dig up new plantings, especially where bonemeal or dried blood has been used. Foxes sometimes dig dens under garden sheds, where they raise their cubs in early summer.

Cats and dogs
The main problem with cats and dogs is their feces, which get underfoot and create an unpleasant smell. Their urine can scorch plants, especially when female dogs urinate on lawns. Cats have a tendency to dig in patches of loose, bare dirt. They are attracted to areas of soft, dry ground when looking for somewhere to defecate. The soiling problem with cats can be reduced by planting densely to deny them open ground.

Woodchucks
Woodchucks, or groundhogs, are widely distributed, powerful rodents, which weigh up to 10 lb (4.5 kg). They hibernate underground in winter, and eat seemingly nonstop to build fat stores during the growing season. Woodchucks can scale or dig under garden fences to eat fruits and entire garden plants. The best defense is an electric garden fence. Woodchucks are difficult to control, and this is best left to a licensed wildlife removal expert.

Mammals and birds *continued*

Mice and rats

Mice eat the seeds of germinating sweet corn, peas, and beans. They also eat crocus corms and orchard fruits, both in gardens and when produce is being stored. They can be controlled by setting mouse traps. If traps are set in gardens, place them under log or brick shelters to reduce the danger to birds. Rats cause similar damage to mice and can also damage root vegetables. They can carry Weil's disease in their urine and so are a particular problem in stored food. They can be controlled by trapping or with poison baits.

Moles

Moles burrow through the soil and patrol their tunnels in search of earthworms and insect grubs. While creating the tunnel system, moles deposit heaps of excavated soil on the surface. This interferes with mowing on lawns and results in an uneven surface when tunnels collapse. Seedlings and low-growing plants can be buried by molehills in flower beds and vegetable plots. Moles can be controlled by trapping (*see p.57*). Ultrasonic sound devices are available for scaring moles away, but they are not always effective.

Deer

Destructive pests in gardens, deer eat the foliage and shoot tips from many plants. The males also rub their antlers against tree trunks, causing damage to the bark and side shoots, which can kill young trees. A robust fence is needed to keep deer out of a garden. There are some plants that are less likely to be eaten, although even these can be damaged when newly planted. Daffodils, hydrangea, and delphinium usually escape damage, as do tough-leaved plants, such as *Yucca* and *Cordyline*. Deer are inquisitive feeders that are attracted to new plantings.

Rabbits

Many vegetables and herbaceous plants are grazed by rabbits. They also kill trees and shrubs by gnawing bark from the stems, particularly during winter. Protect new plantings with wire netting or cloches (*see p.58*) and put tree guards around the base of young trees. If rabbits are a persistent problem, enclose the garden with a rabbit-proof wire netting of 1-in (2.5-cm) mesh. This needs to be 4½ ft (1.4 m) high with the bottom 12 in (30 cm) of the mesh bent outward on the soil surface to stop rabbits from burrowing underneath.

Squirrels

Gray squirrels eat fruits, nuts, sweet corn, flower buds, tulip bulbs, and crocus corms, but their most destructive behavior is stripping bark from trees; where most of the bark has been lost from the trunk circumference, growth above that point dries up and dies. Squirrels may also disfigure lawns and gardens by digging holes and burying nuts, which can sprout into difficult-to-remove tree seedlings. Squirrels can be trapped, but control is ultimately unlikely to be effective unless it is carried out over a much wider area than the size of the average yard.

Pigeons

Pigeons are mainly a problem in vegetable gardens, where they devour the foliage of peas, cabbages, and other brassicas. Damage can occur at any time of year, but often increases in colder weather. Growing vulnerable vegetables under netting will keep pigeons away from the foliage (see p.59). Scaring devices, such as imitation hawks, humming tapes, scarecrows, and glitter strips, are likely to give only temporary protection against the ravages of this bird.

Herons

Herons are not numerous birds but they cover a wide area in their search for food. They soon learn where garden ponds are located and will come down to take fish, frogs, and other pond wildlife. Netting is effective in protecting ponds against these birds, especially those that contain valuable ornamental fish, such as koi carp. A model heron placed at the pond margin is sometimes recommended as a deterrent on the grounds that herons normally prefer to feed alone. This, however, is not a reliable means of protection.

Know your enemy: diseases

Diseases are sicknesses of plants caused by microorganisms known as pathogens, which are most commonly fungi, bacteria, and viruses. The majority of diseases are caused by fungi.

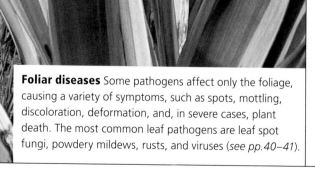

Foliar diseases Some pathogens affect only the foliage, causing a variety of symptoms, such as spots, mottling, discoloration, deformation, and, in severe cases, plant death. The most common leaf pathogens are leaf spot fungi, powdery mildews, rusts, and viruses (*see pp.40–41*).

A serious disease is a rare event and to occur it needs a susceptible host, a virulent pathogen, and a favorable environment. Leaf spot fungi, powdery mildews, and rusts are airborne and spread via spores on air currents or water splashes. Wood decay fungi spread by releasing airborne spores from their brackets or toadstools. They also spread by root contact. Honey fungus is unusual because most of the spread is not by spores but by root contact or by rhizomorphs (bootlaces), a structure it produces to travel from tree to tree in the soil.

Fungus-like organisms such as *Pythium* and *Phytophthora* produce infectious spores that spread in the soil through the water flow. They can also form resting spores that remain dormant in the soil in the absence of a susceptible host. Some species can also produce airborne spores causing leaf blight, twig dieback, and bleeding cankers on susceptible hosts.

Bacteria survive in soil and plant debris. They invade mainly through wounds and are splashed from the soil to the leaves. They spread rapidly in wet weather. Viruses rely on vectoring by insects, nematodes, or mechanical damage to pass them on to new hosts. They may also be seedborne.

Fungi Many different fungi cause the decay of roots or stem base, or branches and stems. They produce annual or perennial fruiting structures, such as toadstools or brackets, most frequently in the fall. The biggest threat to trees and shrubs is honey fungus.

Rots Root and stem rots can be caused by a variety of pathogens, commonly *Phytophthora* (*see p.42*). Affected plants become less vigorous, a tree canopy thins and dieback is widespread, and the root system is reduced and looks brown or black with no obvious fungal growth.

Wilts These diseases are caused by fungi or bacteria that block the vascular tissues, resulting in wilting, stunting, discoloration, stem dieback, or death. The most common wilt diseases are caused by fungi such as *Verticillium* and *Fusarium* (*see p.43*).

Foliar diseases

A number of diseases only affect aerial parts of plants. Some of them, such as downy mildews, can severely affect a plant's health, while others, such as many leaf spots, only spoil its appearance.

Some pathogens, such as rusts and powdery mildews, are easily recognizable because of their typical growth on the leaf surfaces. Others are much more difficult to confirm because they are microscopic in size and the symptoms they produce are not always diagnostic. For example, distortion and stunting caused by many viruses can easily be confused with weedkiller damage, and fungal leaf spots can sometimes be confused with environmental damage. As the number of chemical remedies is limited for the amateur gardener, cultural techniques are key to avoiding the spread of the diseases. Among these are:

- Remove infected plants or parts promptly.
- Avoid overhead watering.
- Keep plants watered, fed, and mulched.
- Remove fallen material at the end of the season.

Fungal leaf spots
Most leaf spots are produced by fungi, but some are caused by bacteria or unsuitable growing conditions. Leaf spot fungi and bacteria thrive in moist weather. Some attack a range of plants, others are host specific. Spots vary in size, shape, and color. They can be disfiguring but unlikely to kill plants. Most fungi survive unfavorable periods. To control, follow the techniques described (*left*) or specific treatments, where available, on pages 64–139.

Downy mildews
These are fungus-like organisms that affect many plants but are usually genus-specific. Off-white mold forms on the underside of leaves, which may be vein-delineated, with corresponding yellow blotches on the upper leaf. Remove diseased plants, improve air circulation, and avoid overhead watering. Lettuce downy mildew can be treated with over-the-counter fungicide labeled for use against downy mildew on lettuce. Spores can persist in soil for years.

Powdery mildews
Powdery mildews include many fungal species that affect a very wide range of plants but usually only infect a group of related plants. Typically, a powdery white coating appears on any part of the plant and infected tissue becomes distorted. The leaves may drop, buds die, or stems die back. Watering during dry periods and improving air circulation by pruning or ventilation will help, as does spraying with an appropriate fungicide.

Viruses

Plants exhibit a range of symptoms when infected by viruses, the most common being chlorotic patches on leaves, often in the forms of mosaics, ring spots, and mottles. Necrotic patches can also result. An infected plant may appear stunted. Viruses are often present in plants propagated from a portion of another plant, such as dahlias and cannas. Transmission is normally by insect vectors or sap. Some are highly contagious and spread by contact between a plant and a surface on which virus particles are present. Viruses cannot be cured, so destroy affected plants.

Rusts

Pustules of powdery orange/brown spores appear on the undersides of leaves and stems with corresponding pale spots on the upper surface. Often leaves fall prematurely. Fungicides are available.

Foliar scabs

Dark green patches appear on the leaves, leading to dead tissues and premature leaf fall. The infections also show as dark sunken spots on fruits or berries, or stem dieback. Treatments are given on pages 64–139.

Smuts

Most smuts are signaled by powdery black masses of spores. Leaf spots appear and organs distort. Smuts produce resilient spores that can persist in the soil for several years. Controls are described on pages 64–139.

Gray mold

The gray mold fungus is very common and affects many plants. It is mainly associated with stem and leaf rots and spreads rapidly by airborne spores, especially in wet conditions (*see p.136*).

Rots and wilts

Diseases that cause symptoms of wilt, stem decay, and root rot are included in this section. These are destructive pathogens that often cause plant death.

The most common root pathogens in gardens are honey fungus and *Phytophthora*. Thorough root examination is often essential to confirm them. Above ground, both pathogens would lead to widespread dieback and collapse of the plant.

Distribution of symptoms may also give some clues as to which disease is causing problems. For example, partial dieback as opposed to overall dieback is often due to a wilt disease rather than a root rot pathogen. The appearance of bracket fungi can also indicate other wood decay pathogens.

As there are no soil sterilants or chemicals available for gardeners to treat these problems, sanitation is important in managing these diseases. Knowing exactly which pathogen has killed your plants helps in choosing suitable resistant replacement plants.

Sclerotinia

Symptoms of *Sclerotinia* include sudden wilting, yellowing of basal leaves, and a brown rot of the stem. This is associated with abundant white mold, often containing hard, black structures called sclerotia. Infected plant material should be destroyed before the sclerotia are released into the soil because they may survive in the ground for many years. For this reason, do not compost the infected plants either. Susceptible plants should not be grown there for up to eight years. The potential host range for this disease is very wide.

Phytophthora

Phytophthora is a microscopic fungus-like organism. There are many species of it, some of which are highly specific, while others have a wide host range. Infected plants most commonly suffer from a root or stem rot, but sometimes have twig and leaf blight. The disease may be associated with bleeding cankers. As result, branches die back. The disease is encouraged by wet conditions. *Phytophthora* can remain dormant in the soil for years. Remove affected plants and the surrounding soil. Improve drainage and keep the infected area free of woody plants for three years.

Verticillium wilt

This wilt disease affects a broad range of edibles and ornamentals. Symptoms of *Verticillium* wilt include individual branches wilting and eventually dying back, often over successive years. Typically, within the vascular tissue of these branches dark streaking is evident. Applying an ammonium-based fertilizer to the root spread may subsequently encourage the production of a new ring of disease-free vascular tissue. The fungus *Verticillium* is soilborne, so the best treatment is to remove badly affected plants and to subsequently replace them with resistant species.

Honey fungus

Honey fungus causes a fatal disease affecting all woody plants. Typical symptoms include thinning of the canopy, branch dieback, or the sudden death of a plant. A white sheet of fungal mycelium will be present between the bark and wood. Sometimes, honey-colored mushrooms with white gills and a collar on the stipe may appear in fall. Destroy infected plants, taking care to remove as much of their root system as possible. Choose plants that are less susceptible to infection, such as *Acer negundo*, beech, boxwood, ivy, laurel, sweet chestnut, and yew.

Fusarium wilt

This fungal disease can affect many herbaceous plants and vegetables. Plants wilt, older leaves look scorched, and a section of stem base reveals a dark discoloration of the tissues. The fungus persists in the soil or in plant debris. Remove infected plants and surrounding soil.

Silver leaf

This fungal disease often affects trees, especially *Prunus*. The leaves become silver, branches die back, and small purple bracket fungi may appear on dead wood. Cutting dying branches in the summer to below where staining ends can save the tree.

Quick diagnosis of the most common symptoms

Listed here are symptoms for the most common pests and diseases described in this book, divided into the plant parts that are most likely to be affected. Bear in mind that some pests and diseases present more than one symptom.

If you can't find what you are looking for on pages 44–49, but know what your plant is, refer to the specific group, such as roses on pages 86–87, *Prunus* on pages 124–125, and potatoes on pages 116–117, or check the index. Sometimes a disease or pest relating to one specific plant will also attack other plants. For example, hollyhock rust attacks hollyhocks (*Althaea rosea*), but also lavatera and other related genera. Lists of any such plants are given at the start of their relative section.

Leaves
Symptoms: Leaf spots generally round and spreading over leaf veins; also elongate spots on stems
Potential diseases: Fungal leaf spots (*p.40*)
See the following:
Arbutus leaf spots (*p.70*)
Brassica dark and light leaf spots (*p.114*)
Brassica ring spot (*p.114*)
Celery late blight (*p.121*)

Cherry leaf scorch (*p.124*)
Cherry leaf spot (*p.124*)
Currant and gooseberry leaf spot (*p.126*)
Dahlia smut (*p.103*)
Escallonia leaf spots (*p.77*)
Hellebore leaf blotch (*p.96*)
Iris leaf spot (*p.101*)
Ivy leaf spot (*p.84*)
Lily disease (*p.100*)
Mulberry leaf spot (*p.127*)
Pansy leaf spots (*p.99*)
Rhododendron leaf spot (*p.83*)
Robinia decline (*p.74*)
Rose black spot (*p.87*)
Strawberry leaf spot (*p.129*)
Tar spot of *Acer* (*p.70*)
Yucca leaf spot (*p.81*)

———————————————————

Symptoms: Spots often angular because they are limited by leaf veins; color is usually uniform; spots may initially be water-soaked
Potential pest/disease: Leaf and bud eelworms, bacterial leaf spots
See the following:
Bean halo blight (*p.113*)
Delphinium bacterial leaf spot (*p.95*)

Leaf and bud eelworms (*p.91*)
Mulberry bacterial blight (*p.127*)

———————————————————

Symptoms: Irregular brown/black spots or blotches on the leaves; spots may coalesce and leaves fall prematurely; branches or stems may die back
Potential disease: Leaf blight
See the following:
Bean anthracnose (*p.113*)
Bean chocolate spot (*p.113*)
Boxwood blight (*p.80*)
Dogwood anthracnose (*p.71*)
Holly leaf blight (*p.77*)
Holly leaf miner (*p.76*)
Horse chestnut leaf blotch (*p.72*)
Leek white tip (*p.120*)
Lupine anthracnose (*p.94*)
Peony gray mold (*p.96*)
Plane anthracnose (*p.74*)
Potato late blight and tomato blight (*p.117 and p.119*)
Quince leaf blight (*p.74*)
Rhododendron leaf blight and dieback (*p.83*)
Willow anthracnose (*p.75*)
Willow black canker (*p.75*)

Tar spot of Acer

Hellebore leaf blotch

Rhododendron leaf blight and dieback

Symptoms: Blackish-brown discolored areas, often sharply divided from uninfested parts by larger leaf veins
Potential pest: Leaf and bud eelworm (*p.91*)

Symptoms: Fine, pale mottling on the upper surface, which gradually becomes yellowish-brown
Potential pests: Leafhoppers, red spider mites, thrips
See the following:
Conifer red spider mite (*p.76*)
Fruit tree red spider mite (*p.111*)
Gladiolus thrips (*p.100*)
Greenhouse leafhopper (*p.138*)
Greenhouse thrips (*p.137*)
Pea thrips (*p.112*)
Pieris lacebug (*p.80*)
Privet thrips (*p.76*)
Red spider mite (*p.136*)
Rose leafhopper (*p.87*)
Sage leafhopper (*p.131*)

Symptoms: Dark green patches on tree leaves leading to dead tissue and premature leaf fall
Potential disease: Tree scabs (*p.69*)
See the following:
Apple and pear scabs (*p.69*)

Symptoms: Chlorotic patches, often appearing in the form of mosaics, ringspots, and mottles; distortion of leaves
Potential disease: Viruses (*p.41*)
See the following:
Camellia yellow mottle virus (*p.82*)
Canna viruses (*p.97*)
Cucumber mosaic virus (*p.119*)
Greenhouse viruses (*p.139*)
Hellebore black death (*p.96*)
Lettuce viruses (*p.118*)
Nicotiana viruses (*p.99*)
Orchid viruses (*p.139*)
Parsnip viruses (*p.117*)
Passion flower viruses (*p.85*)
Petunia viruses (*p.99*)
Raspberry leaf and bud mite (*p.128*)
Rose viruses (*p.87*)
Strawberry viruses (*p.129*)
Tomato viruses (*p.119*)

Symptoms: Leaves are distorted and filled with powdery black masses of spores
Potential disease: Smuts (*p.41*)
See the following:
Anemone smut (*p.101*)

Symptoms: Off-white mold on the underside of leaves and corresponding yellow, purple, or brown blotches on the upper leaves
Potential disease: Downy mildew (*p.40*)

See the following:
Brassica downy mildew (*p.114*)
Grape erinose mite (*p.127*)
Hebe downy mildew (*p.81*)
Impatiens downy mildew (*p.98*)
Lettuce downy mildew (*p.118*)
Nicotiana downy mildew (*p.99*)
Pansy downy mildew (*p.99*)
Pea downy mildew (*p.112*)

Symptoms: Powdery white coating with infected tissue becoming distorted and leaves may drop
Potential disease: Powdery mildew (*p.40*)
See the following:
Acanthus powdery mildew (*p.96*)
American gooseberry mildew (*p.127*)
Bay powdery mildew (*p.130*)
Cucumber powdery mildew (*p.119*)
Delphinium powdery mildew (*p.95*)
Geranium (cranesbill) powdery mildew (*p.94*)
Honeysuckle powdery mildew (*p.85*)
Oak powdery mildew (*p.73*)
Pea powdery mildew (*p.112*)
Raspberry powdery mildew (*p.128*)
Rhododendron powdery mildew (*p.83*)
Sweet pea powdery mildew (*p.98*)

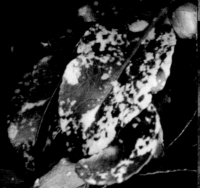

Rose leafhopper | Camellia yellow mottle virus

Acanthus powdery mildew

Quick diagnosis of the most common symptoms *continued*

Leaves *continued*

Symptoms: White waxy bands of eggs on the underside of evergreen leaves, often with heavy coating of sooty mold on upper leaf surface
Potential pest: Cottony cushion scale (*p.66*)

Symptom: White waxy clusters on greenhouse plants
Potential pests: Fluted scale (*p.137*), mealybug (*p.138*)
See the following:
Phormium mealybug (*p.92*)

Symptom: White chalky eruptions on the underside of leaves
Potential disease: White rust (*p.109*)

Symptoms: Soft-bodied insects covered by shells or scales; foliage sometimes sticky, with sooty molds
Potential pest: Scale insects (*p.32*)
See the following:
Brown scale (*p.110*)
Cottony cushion scale (*p.66*)
Euonymus scale (*p.80*)
Fluted scale (*p.137*)
Hemispherical scale (*p.137*)
Horse chestnut scale (*p.72*)
Hydrangea scale (*p.80*)
Oleander scale (*p.137*)
Soft scale (*p.137*)
Wisteria scale (*p.85*)

Symptoms: Abnormal growths or galls on foliage
Potential cause: Various pests or fungi
See the following:
Acer pimple gall (*p.70*)
Azalea and camellia leaf galls (*p.82*)
Bay sucker (*p.130*)
Boxwood sucker (*p.80*)
Elm gall mite (*p.71*)
Eucalyptus gall wasp (*p.71*)
Gall mites (*p.66*)
Gleditsia gall midge (*p.78*)
Lime nail gall mite (*p.72*)
Oak gall wasps (*p.73*)
Peach leaf curl (*p.124*)
Plum gall mite (*p.125*)
Violet gall midge (*p.93*)
Walnut gall mite (*p.74*)
Willow bean gall sawfly (*p.75*)

Symptoms: Pustules of powdery yellow/orange/brown/off-white spores on the undersides of leaves with corresponding pale spots on the upper surface; often leaves fall prematurely
Potential disease: Rust (*p.41*)
See the following:
Antirrhinum rust (*p.97*)
Bean rust (*p.113*)
Chrysanthemum brown rust (*p.95*)
Chrysanthemum white rust (*p.95*)
Fuchsia rust (*p.79*)
Hollyhock rust (*p.97*)

Iris rust (*p.101*)
Mahonia rust (*p.81*)
Mint rust (*p.131*)
Pear rust (*p.123*)
Pelargonium (geranium) rust (*p.94*)
Periwinkle rust (*p.97*)
Raspberry rust (*p.129*)
Rhododendron rust (*p.83*)
Rose rust (*p.87*)

Symptoms: Leaves turn silver and branches die back
Potential disease: Silverleaf disease (*p.43*)

Symptom: Twisting white or brown lines or mines causing brown, dried-up blotches in the leaves
Potential pest: Leaf miners (*p.32*)
See the following:
Allium leaf miner (*p.120*)
Apple leaf-mining moth (*p.122*)
Beet leaf miner (*p.121*)
Celery leaf miner (*p.121*)
Chrysanthemum leaf miner (*p.95*)
Holly leaf miner (*p.76*)
Holm oak leaf miner (*p.73*)
Horse chestnut leaf-mining moth (*p.72*)
Laburnum leaf miner (*p.78*)
Leek moth (*p.120*)
Lilac leaf miner (*p.78*)
Pyracantha leaf miner (*p.79*)
Sempervivum leaf miner (*p.92*)

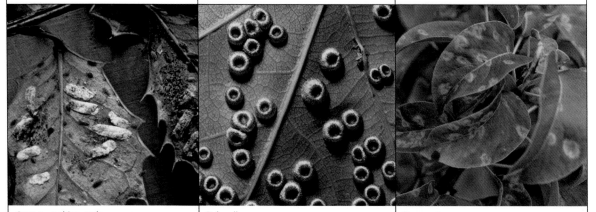

Cottony cushion scale | Oak gall wasps | Pear rust

Symptom: Foliage being eaten
Potential pests: Beetles (*p.30*), butterfly, moth, and sawfly larvae (*p.32*), mammals (*pp.35–7*), slugs and snails (*p.34*)
See the following:
Asparagus beetle (*p.121*)
Berberis sawfly (*p.78*)
Brassica flea beetles (*p.114*)
Cabbage white butterflies (*pp.98, 115*)
Colorado potato beetle (*p.108*)
Cotoneaster webber moth (*p.79*)
Elephant hawk moth (*p.79*)
Figwort weevil (*p.79*)
Geranium (cranesbill) sawfly (*p.94*)
Geum sawfly (*p.93*)
Gooseberry sawflies (*p.127*)
Grasshoppers on mint (*p.130*)
Gypsy moth caterpillar (*p.73*)
Iris sawfly (*p.101*)
Lily leaf beetle (*p.100*)
Mullein moth (*p.92*)
Pea and bean weevil (*p.112*)
Pear and cherry slugworm (*p.123*)
Rose slugworm sawfly (*p.86*)
Solomon's seal sawfly (*p.92*)
Tomato fruitworm (*p.118*)
Tortrix moth (*p.90*; greenhouse *p.138*)
Viburnum beetle (*p.81*)
Vine weevil—adults (*p.34*)
Water lily beetle (*p.93*)
Willow leaf beetle (*p.75*)
Winter moth (*p.110*)

Symptom: Regular-sized pieces of leaf missing with smooth outline
Potential pest: Leafcutter bee (*p.31*)

Symptom: Holes on leaves on *Prunus*
Potential diseases: Bacterial canker (*p.124*), bacterial leaf spots, cherry leaf spot (*p.124*), fungal leaf spots (*p.40*)

Symptoms: Sudden wilting of the leaves, yellowing of basal leaves, a brown rot of the stem and abundant white mold
Potential disease: *Sclerotinia* (*p.42*)

Symptoms: Leaves wilt and stems die back; staining may or may not be visible in the stem tissues while roots are initially alive
Potential diseases: Wilts
See the following:
Clematis wilt (*p.84*)
Dutch elm disease (*p.71*)
Fusarium wilt (*p.43*)
Verticillium wilt (*p.43*)

Symptoms: Leaves wilt and die; stems die back; no staining is visible in the stem tissues, but roots are rotted
Potential diseases: Root rots
See the following:
Damping off (*p.139*)
Honey fungus (*p.43*)

Pansy sickness (*p.99*)
Phytophthora root rot (*p.42*)
Wisteria dieback (*p.85*)

Symptoms: Leaves wilt on hot days, recovering overnight
Potential problems: Clubroot (*p.109*), root aphids (*p.33*)
See the following:
Lettuce root aphid (*p.118*)
Root mealybugs (*p.138*)

Symptoms: Tree leaves wilt and turn brown but remain attached to tree
Potential diseases: Cherry leaf scorch (*p.124*), Fireblight (*p.111*)

Symptoms: Dense colony of variously colored sap-sucking insects on shoot tips and leaves, excreting a sticky honeydew
Potential pests: Aphids (see *p.31*), suckers, whitefly
See the following:
Beech woolly aphid (*p.70*)
Black bean aphid (*p.113*)
Cabbage whitefly (*p.115*)
Cherry blackfly (*p.124*)
Currant blister aphid (*p.126*)
Cypress aphid (*p.76*)
Eucalyptus sucker (*p.71*)
Greenhouse aphids (*p.139*)
Greenhouse whitefly (*p.136*)
(*continued on p.48*)

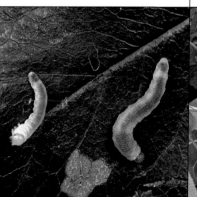

Rose slugworm sawfly

Sclerotinia

Greenhouse whitefly

Quick diagnosis of the most common symptoms *continued*

Leaves *continued*
Honeysuckle aphid (*p.85*)
Lupine aphid (*p.94*)
Mealy cabbage aphid (*p.115*)
Mealy plum aphid (*p.125*)
Pear bedstraw aphid (*p.123*)
Plum leaf-curl aphid (*p.125*)
Rose aphid (*p.86*)
Viburnum whitefly (*p.81*)
Water lily aphid (*p.93*)

Flowers and buds
Symptoms: Color breaking
Potential disease: Virus (*p.41*)
See the following:
Petunia viruses (*p.99*)
Camellia yellow mottle virus (*p.82*)

Symptom: Flowers and/or buds with fluffy gray mold growth
Potential disease: Gray mold *p.136*)
See the following:
Lily disease (*p.100*)

Symptoms: Anthers become swollen and distorted and are covered with masses of black spores
Potential disease: Smuts (*p.41*)
See the following:
Dianthus smut (*p.95*)

Symptom: Flower buds wither or open unevenly

Potential pests: Plant bugs (*p.31*), New York aster daisy mite (*p.93*)

Symptom: Fruit tree flowers wilt and turn brown
Potential disease: Blossom wilt (*p.111*)

Symptom: Abnormal growths or galls on buds
Potential pests: Gall midges, gall mites (*p.66*)
See the following:
Black currant big bud mites (*p.126*)
Broom gall mite (*p.78*)
Hemerocallis gall midge (*p.94*)

Symptom: Flower buds devoured on fruit trees and bushes
Potential pest: Birds (*p.111*)

Fruit
Symptoms: Dark blotches or spots on fruits and berries
Potential disease: Tree scabs (*p.69*)
See the following:
Quince leaf blight (*p.74*)

Symptom: Rings of buff spores on fruits
Potential disease: Brown rot (*p.123*)

Symptoms: Fruits with fluffy gray mold growth or with small white rings sometimes associated with gray mold growth
Potential disease: Gray mold (*p.136*)
See the following:
Tomato ghost spot (*p.118*)
Strawberry gray mold (*p.129*)

Symptoms: Fruits with a white or off-white fungal coating
Potential disease: Powdery mildew (*p.40*)
See the following:
American gooseberry mildew (*p.127*)

See also fruit trees (*pp.122–125*), soft fruit (*pp.126–127*), raspberries and strawberries (*pp.128–129*)

Trunks, branches, and stems
Symptom: Abnormal twig proliferation leading to reduction in flowering
Potential disease: Witches' broom (*p.68*)

Symptom: Dead sections on branches, main trunks, or stems
Potential diseases: Blossom wilt (*p.111*), cankers (*p.68*), fireblight (*p.111*)

Dianthus smut

Brown rot

Witches' broom

See the following:
Apple and pear canker (*p.123*)
Bacterial canker (*p.124*)
Poplar canker (*p.75*)
Rose canker and dieback (*p.87*)

Symptoms: Branches dying as a result of root or stem rot; fungal growth may or may not be apparent on dying stems or roots
Potential diseases: Nectria canker (*p.67*), gray mold (*p.41*), honey fungus (*p.43*), *Phytophthora* (*p.42*), *Sclerotinia* (*p.42*), wood decay fungi (*p.69*)
See the following:
Lavender gray mold (*p.131*)
Peony gray mold (*p.96*)
Robinia decline (*p.74*)
Roses (*p.86*)
Snowdrop gray mold (*p.103*)
Strawberry gray mold (*p.129*)
Tulip fire (*p.103*)
Wisteria dieback (*p.85*)
Yew Phytophthora root rot (*p.77*)

Symptom: Bleeding on stems or branches
Potential diseases: Cankers (*p.68*), root rots
See the following:
Bacterial canker (*p.124*)
Coryneum canker (*p.68*)
Honey fungus (*p.43*)

Horse chestnut bleeding canker (*p.72*)
Phytophthora (*p.42*)

Symptoms: Branches wilt and eventually die back; staining is visible in the conducting tissue below the bark
Potential diseases: Wilts
See the following:
Dutch elm disease (*p.71*)
Fusarium wilt (*p.43*)
Verticillium wilt (*p.43*)

Symptoms: Stems covered with slimy growth and die back
Potential disease: Slime flux
See the following:
Clematis slime flux (*p.84*)

Symptoms: Small brownish-black shells attached to the stems, sometimes with sticky foliage
Potential pest: Scale insects
See the following:
Brown scale (*p.110*)
Euonymus scale (*p.80*)
Hemispherical and soft scales (*p.137*)
Horse chestnut scale (*p.72*)
Hydrangea scale (*p.80*)
Wisteria scale (*p.85*)

Roots, bulbs, and tubers
Symptoms: Root rot causing branches to die back

Potential diseases: Honey fungus (*p.43*), *Phytophthora* (*p.42*)
See the following:
Damping off (*p.139*)
Pansy sickness (*p.99*)
Roses (*p.86*)
Wisteria dieback (*p.85*)

Symptom: Large woody gall on roots
Potential disease: Crown gall (*p.68*)

Symptom: Roots thickened and distorted into a swollen mass
Potential disease: Clubroot (*p.109*)

Symptom: Small holes in tubers, onion bulbs, or other root vegetables
Potential pests: Slugs (*p.34*), wireworms (*p.108*)

Symptoms: Roots eaten and plants often wilt
Potential pest: Cutworms (*p.108*)
See the following:
Cabbage root fly (*p.115*)
Carrot fly (*p.121*)
Chafer grubs (*p.104*)
Leatherjackets (*p.104*)
Onion fly (*p.120*)
Vine weevil grubs (*pp.33 and 138*)

See also Bulbs, corms, tubers, and rhizomes (*pp.100–103*)

Apple and pear canker

Honey fungus

Crown gall

Controlling pests and diseases

Not everything in the garden is perfect, and sooner or later pests and diseases will become apparent. Some can be tolerated, but others may require action to prevent them from becoming a more severe problem. This can be achieved by various means, including the use of insecticides and fungicides, as well as natural enemies, physical barriers, and other nonchemical treatments. Correct identification of the cause of the problem is essential so that appropriate measures can be taken at the right time.

How chemicals work

Select chemicals depending on the plant, pest, or disease that needs to be treated. Sometimes a combination of methods might be required to eradicate the problem. Use chemicals only if the damage could be significant and cannot be minimized using other techniques, such as those listed on pages 56–63.

Choosing the right chemical

Only use a chemical when it is recommended for the purpose you have in mind. It is illegal to use a pesticide (fungicide or insecticide) on plants, pests, or diseases not listed on the label. For example, a chemical labeled to control rusts on ornamentals should not be used to control other diseases on other ornamentals. Try the chemical on a few leaves first to make sure there are no adverse effects on the plant.

Only use chemicals when necessary. Many pests and diseases can be kept under control by good cultivation techniques, as described on pages 6–23. In addition, encouraging beneficial creatures (*see pp.60–63*) can be an effective alternative to using chemical sprays.

Read the labels of organic treatments. Be aware that pyrethrum, for example, is deadly to fish and can harm beneficial insects. Some products, such as insecticidal soap, are not registered for use on food plants.

Pick caterpillars off plants Picking caterpillars off lightly infested plants by hand is a more sensible way of controlling them than spraying. If the infestation is severe, consider applying a contact insecticide labeled for use on the specific plant for the pest you want to control.

Ladybugs These beetles are the best-known natural predators of aphids. Lacewing larvae, hoverflies, robins, and some midges also feed on aphids. Attract aphid eaters by feeding birds or growing small-flowered nectar plants like Queen Anne's lace.

Application methods

Chemicals vary in the way they work and it is important to know if you are using a contact or systemic pesticide. This influences how and when you apply the chemical.

Contact pesticides only kill insects or fungi that are hit by the spray or crawl over sprayed leaves. It is important to spray plants thoroughly, including both sides of the leaves.

Systemic pesticides are absorbed into the plant and are translocated to parts of plants that have not been treated. They kill fungi within the plant tissues and are also useful in killing sap-feeding insects, which are difficult to reach with contact insecticides.

Preventive pesticides form a protective barrier on the surface of plants that stops fungi or bacteria from penetrating. Apply them thoroughly to the plant and before infection or infestation occurs. A few systemic fungicides also have some protective action.

Most insecticides available to gardeners have a broad spectrum of activity. This means that most insects, including both pests and beneficial insects, may be killed if insecticide is applied, so always follow the package directions carefully. Chemicals may be available as concentrated liquid sprays or drenches, ready-to-use sprays and pump guns, dusts, and pellets.

Liquids Liquid concentrate is cheap but needs to be diluted to the volume required and needs special equipment for application. Ready-to-use sprays are already diluted at the appropriate concentrations, but they are only useful if small areas need to be treated.

Dusts Only a few contact chemicals are available as dusts. Although they leave an unsightly deposit, they are easy to apply on the targeted organism and little is wasted as dusts are used directly from the package. For example, sulfur dusts kill powdery mildew spores as they germinate.

Pellets A few pests can be controlled by pellets, such as slugs and snails. Follow the manufacturer's instructions and scatter pellets only where children and pets cannot eat them and be poisoned. For extra safety, and to protect wildlife as well, place pellets within bait houses.

Using chemicals

Use garden chemicals with care to minimize any adverse effect they may have on the environment. Their safe storage and disposal is equally important, although this is quite often overlooked by the gardener. For full effectiveness and safety, follow the instructions on the label. Safety rules should also apply to the equipment you use to treat plants.

Mixing and applying chemicals

Follow the instructions on the manufacturer's label and apply the chemical at the stated rate and as described, as this is often crucial to control the pest or disease. It is illegal to mix your own blends, including using dish soap to kill aphids. Many chemicals are also incompatible. When a commercial product contains both an insecticide and a fungicide, use an alternative product if only a pest or disease has been a problem on the plant to be treated.

Measuring When making up solutions from concentrates, use water from a container rather than diluting directly from a faucet or hose. Avoid making up more than necessary to avoid having to dispose of the surplus.

Mixing Pour concentrated pesticide in the sprayer already partially filled with water. Rinse the measurer and use the rinsed-out water to make up the solution. Make up to the final volume and close the container before mixing and applying the chemical.

Applying Spray the plants, including stems, buds, and both surfaces of leaves. Avoid excessive run-off. Apply at dusk or early morning on dry, still days to avoid scorching, spare beneficial insects, and optimize chemical action.

Equipment If only small areas need to be treated—for example, plants in a greenhouse—a ready-to-use spray might be the best option. A cheaper alternative is to use a small hand-pump sprayer, which you can keep refilling when necessary. When large areas need to be treated, you might need to buy special equipment, such as a sprayer with an external pump. Watering cans fitted with a dribble bar are particularly suitable for soil drenching. As for all pesticide applicators, they should be clearly labeled and used for no other purposes. Especially do not use the same container for weedkillers and pesticides as your plants could end up being severely damaged.

Storage Pesticide products are best stored at an even temperature. Concentrates will store for two years or more if kept in cool, dark conditions. Diluted concentrates can become ineffective after just 24 hours, so remember to only dilute enough for one day's use.

Safety For safety reasons, it is illegal to store pesticides that are unlabeled and not in their original container. Ready-to-use sprays can be more convenient for smaller areas, requiring no mixing and keeping just as long. Never dispose of surplus pesticide down drains, sewers, ditches, or in watercourses because of the risk of contaminating water and harming wildlife. Instead, dilute small quantities and spray onto permitted plants according to the manufacturer's instructions. Once rinsed thoroughly, place empty containers in household waste, rather than recycling them. Add the rinsing to the final spray solution or dispose of it as for surplus pesticides. When pesticides are withdrawn from the market, usually for economic reasons, there is a grace period of one to two years in which to use up stock. Contact your municipality's waste management department for disposal of larger quantities of pesticides. Find more information at www.epa.gov/epahome/hotline.htm.

Lock pesticides away Store them in a dark, cool place, out of reach of children, pets, and wildlife, preferably locked in a garden shed or garage, not in the house. Keep chemicals in their original containers tightly closed and clearly labeled. Dispose of obsolete products safely.

Use gardening gloves Take care not to spill any chemicals, and wear gloves when handling them. Wash your hands and face immediately if you accidentally splash chemicals on them. Take particular care if products bear a warning label with the words "harmful" or "irritant."

Use a designated watering can Thoroughly wash watering cans and sprayers after use. Even small residues of weedkillers can harm plants. Dispose of rinsed water safely, not into drains or near ponds and watercourses. Do not mix different products.

Nonchemical controls: traps

Some traps can be used to reduce the numbers of certain pests, while other traps are used to monitor pest numbers and indicate the appropriate time to take additional control measures.

Setting traps

Trapping is a technique that can be used successfully in the garden against various invertebrate pests, such as slugs and snails, as well as some mammals. Setting traps for mammals, such as rats, mice, moles, gray squirrels, and rabbits, requires a bit of knowledge about the animals' behavior patterns, since careful placement of traps in places frequented by the animals will increase the chances of success. Some traps are designed to kill the animal outright, while others are cages that capture the animal alive for subsequent humane disposal, which is not a job for the squeamish. Trapping and disposing of invertebrate pests is an easier matter.

Sticky traps Yellow plastic sheets covered with a nondrying glue capture pests such as whitefly, thrips, and fungus gnats in greenhouses. These traps can be used to detect greenhouse whitefly before plants become too heavily infested for biological control to be effective.

Grease bands Apply grease bands to the trunks and stakes of fruit trees in the fall. The wingless female of winter moths emerge from pupae in the soil and crawl up the trunk to lay eggs on the branches. Sticky bands ensure that some females fail to make the journey.

Slug traps Slugs and snails hide in dark damp places during the day. Placing pieces of cardboard, tiles, or similar materials on the soil provides them with hiding places from which they can be removed. Slugs can also be lured into beer-filled containers sunk into the soil, where they drown.

Wasp traps Wasps are attracted to sweet substances, especially in mid- to late summer. Make a trap by half-filling a jar with water and jam. Cover the top with paper with a ½-in (1-cm) hole in the center. Attracted by the fermenting contents, wasps will enter the jar and drown.

Pheromone traps Pheromones are produced by insects to attract a mate. For some pests, such as codling moth, use traps containing the attractant scent. Only males are caught, but the traps record the flight period for more accurate timing of sprays against newly hatched caterpillars.

Mole traps Several mole traps are available, such as the Duffus trap shown here. Set and place the trap in the mole's tunnel and then cover to exclude light. Check the trap at least once a day. Reset it in another part of the tunnel system if the mole keeps pushing soil into the trap.

Rabbit traps Entice rabbits into humane traps (live cage traps) by scattering carrots inside and around the trap. If you have a severe problem with rabbits, consider calling a licensed professional wildlife removal company for advice and assistance.

Nonchemical controls: barriers and repellents

Pest damage can sometimes be avoided or reduced by placing a physical barrier in the affected area that excludes the pest or presents a surface that the pest is reluctant to cross.

Where to use barriers

Barriers may not enhance the appearance of a garden, but they can be an effective means of keeping pests away from plants. Barriers, such as those described here, are more frequently used in vegetable gardens than in flower borders. They are particularly useful for protecting plants at vulnerable stages in their growth, such as seedlings, transplants, young shoots on herbaceous plants, and new plantings. Once plants have made some growth and become established, it is usually safe to remove the protective covers. It is undesirable to leave plants covered up for too long as the covers may reduce light, resulting in decidedly weak and spindly plants. They can also become overcrowded or run out of space.

Copper tape Slugs and snails have an aversion to copper and when confronted by a copper strip fixed around a pot or tub will usually turn away, rather than cross it. These pests can also be deterred by standing plant containers on mats impregnated with copper salts.

Tree guards Rabbits gnaw the bark from the trunks and stem bases on trees and shrubs, especially in the winter months. This can be fatal for the plant if most of the bark is lost. Protect woody plants by placing a collar or tree guard around the base of the trunk.

Rabbit deterrent Rabbits are attracted to new plantings. To keep them at bay, place covers over the plants or erect a barrier of wire netting around the plants. This enables new plants to get established and to survive rabbit grazing when the covers are removed.

Protect young plants Slugs and snails can quickly demolish seedlings and soft young shoots, which can be protected by placing cloches, made from plastic bottles from which the top and bottom have been removed, over the seedlings. Remove before they get too leggy.

Fine mesh netting Place finely woven floating row cover over vegetables such as carrots and brassicas to exclude the egg-laying females of pests, such as carrot fly and cabbage root fly, for which there are no pesticides available for garden use. Keep in place until fall.

Brassica collars Cabbage root fly lays its eggs in the soil close to the stems of its host plants. Place homemade or purchased collars about 5 in (12 cm) across around the base of brassica transplants to stop flies from placing eggs nearby. Eggs laid on the collars dry up and fail to hatch.

Scarecrows While scarecrows can add to the fun of a garden, they are usually of little benefit in protecting plants from birds and other pests. Unless there is some real danger associated with a scaring device, birds, rabbits, and deer quickly become accustomed to it and ignore it.

Beneficial creatures

Not all insects and other garden wildlife are pests! Some are of real benefit to gardeners as pollinators of flowers or as predators or parasites of pests.

When is a pest not a pest?

Most of the fruits we grow need pollen to be transferred from one flower to another in order for the fruit to develop. Many vegetables and ornamental flowers also require pollination so they can set seed. Many insects can perform this task, but bees are particularly efficient as pollinators.

Animals become garden pests when they are sufficiently abundant to have an adverse effect on plants. In the absence of natural checks, such as predators, parasites, and diseases, pests rapidly increase in numbers. Fortunately, most gardens have an array of large and small animals that feed on pest species. These beneficial animals are not always effective in preventing pest infestations, but without them, the situation could be a lot worse. The most effective predators or parasites are those that target specific pests.

Bumblebees
Bumblebees are social insects that live in nests, usually underground but also at ground level or in bird nest boxes. They are valuable in the garden as they will pollinate flowers during weather when honeybees stay in their hives. Each nest contains a queen bee and up to 200 worker bees. The nest is initiated in late spring by the queen and builds up to peak strength in late summer. Male bees and next year's queens are produced in late summer, after which the colony dies out. Only young queens overwinter.

Honeybees
Like bumblebees, honeybees are social insects headed by a queen bee, but with colonies of up to 60,000 workers. These semidomesticated insects are kept by beekeepers in hives. Honeybees differ from bumblebees by surviving the winter as an active colony, so large numbers of worker bees are available for pollination duty in spring when fruit trees blossom. In addition to their role as pollinators, honeybees provide us with other products, such as honey and beeswax.

Lacewings

Some lacewings have green bodies that are ⅜–¾ in (8–22 mm) long, but other species are black or brown. The adult insects feed on pollen and nectar, while their larvae are voracious predators of aphids and other small insects. Lacewings have long, threadlike antennae and are named after their attractive, multiveined wings. The larvae have elongate bodies and a pair of sharp curved jaws with which they seize their prey. Some lacewing larvae disguise themselves by covering their backs with a layer of sucked-out aphid skins.

Hoverfly larvae

The legless hoverfly maggots have flattened bodies up to ½ in (12 mm) long, and are often found on aphid-infested plants during the summer. A single larva can devour up to 600 aphids before it is fully fed and ready to pupate. The colors of adult hoverflies are often mainly black with yellow bands or other markings on their abdomens. Their name comes from their ability to hover in flight. Like lacewings, adult hoverflies feed on nectar and pollen.

Flower bugs

These predatory insects, also known as anthocorid bugs, are ⅛–¼ in (3–5 mm) long. The adult flower bugs and their nymphs insert needlelike mouthparts into the eggs or bodies of small insects and mites in order to suck out the contents. They are active from spring to fall, spending the winter hidden in sheltered places. Some flower bug species live mainly on trees and can be useful predatorsof pests on fruit trees, such as aphids, suckers, and red spider mites.

Beneficial creatures *continued*

Frogs and toads
These amphibians eat a wide range of insects, slugs, woodlice, and other small creatures. They do most of their feeding at night during spring to fall. A garden pond provides somewhere for frogs and toads to breed in the spring.

Ladybugs
Both the adult beetles and larvae of most ladybugs are predatory insects. Many ladybugs prey on aphids, but others specialize in feeding on scale insects, mealybugs, or red spider mites. The adults are often red or yellow with varying numbers of black spots; others are brown or orange and have white spots. The larvae, however, have less distinctive markings. They are black with orange or white markings and are up to ½ in (12 mm) long. Ladybug larvae can eat up to 500 aphids, and probably as many again when they become adult insects.

Shrews
Shrews are small mammals that are largely nocturnal and so not often seen. They eat large numbers of insects, spiders, worms, and slugs. Shrews have characteristic pointed snouts that separate them from similar-sized mice and voles.

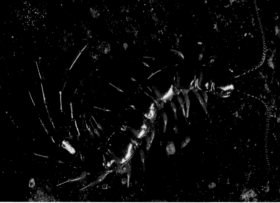

Centipedes
These insects have elongate, segmented bodies that are orange-brown or pale yellow. Each body segment bears a single pair of legs, unlike millipedes, which have two pairs per segment. The front pair of legs curves forward and is modified to act as jaws. Some centipedes live and hunt for small creatures on the soil surface. They are up to 1¼ in (30 mm) long. Other centipedes, however, live in the soil and these often have much longer and more slender bodies.

Robin
Robins are found throughout North America, migrating north in early spring to nest and feed on worms, insects, berries, and rose hips. Up to 20 percent of their diet consists of earthworms, which they catch by plunging their beaks into the soil. Their red breasts and blue eggs, their reputation as a symbol of spring, and their beautiful dawn and sunset songs make robins welcome backyard visitors. They nest in trees and shrubs and can raise two broods of three to five chicks during the summer months.

Biological controls

Biological control is the use of a natural enemy to control a pest. Some parasites, predators, and pathogenic nematodes can be purchased for this purpose.

Predators, such as ladybugs and larvae of hoverflies and lacewings, capture their prey and kill it quickly.

Parasitic wasps and flies lay eggs on or inside the eggs or bodies of a suitable host insect or other invertebrate animal. They hatch into larvae that initially cause no obvious harm to the host insect, which continues feeding and growing. Eventually the parasite larvae destroy the host insect's vital organs and, at that point, the host insect is killed and the parasite larvae emerge and pupate.

Pathogenic nematodes are microscopic wormlike animals that invade the bodies of various pests, mainly those that live in the soil. These nematodes release bacteria that infect the host animal with a fatal disease. Such nematodes are used against vine weevil grubs, chafer grubs, leatherjackets and slugs.

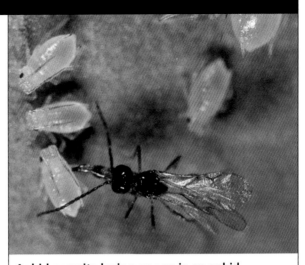

Aphid parasite laying an egg in an aphid
Parasitic wasps, such as *Aphidius* and *Praon* species, lay single eggs inside the bodies of young aphids. The aphids continue feeding and growing but are unable to reproduce. The parasite larva developing inside the aphid eventually kills it. Parasitized aphids become brown or black and abnormally inflated and rounded shortly before they die. The parasite pupates inside or under the dead aphid's body.

Pathogenic nematodes
These microscopic eelworms or nematodes are watered into the soil or potting medium to control pests, such as slugs and vine weevil grubs, or lawn pests, such as chafer grubs and leatherjackets. Different species of nematodes are required for these pests. The nematodes, which give the pests a fatal bacterial infection, need to be applied to moist soil at a time when soil temperatures are sufficiently high to allow the nematodes to be active during spring to early fall.

Predatory aphid midge
The larvae of a tiny fly, *Aphidoletes aphidimyza*, prey on greenfly and other aphids. The orange larvae, which are up to ⅛ in (3 mm) long, insert their mouthparts into the leg joints of aphids and then suck out the body contents. Each midge larva will control about 60 aphids before it then goes into the soil to pupate. This biological control can be purchased for use in greenhouses, but the fly also occurs in gardens on aphid-infested plants throughout the summer.

Trees, shrubs, and climbers

Trees can be difficult to treat if they are affected by a pest or disease, quite simply because of their size. However, many problems on young trees can be prevented—or controlled—by maintaining good hygiene and tackling any problems as soon as they become apparent. The same goes for shrubs and climbers, especially by ensuring that, where necessary, you prune your plants regularly and at the right time to prevent overcrowding.

Trees, shrubs, and climbers: general pests and diseases

The pests and diseases described on these pages and overleaf can affect many of the plants found in this section. Host-specific pests and diseases are described in their relevant groups.

The plant divisions in this chapter are:
- Trees (*see pp.70–75*)
- Conifers and hedges (*see pp.76–77*)
- Shrubs (*see pp.78–81*)
- Azaleas, camellias, and rhododendrons (*see pp.82–83*)
- Climbers (*see pp.84–85*)
- Roses (*see pp.86–87*)

Gall mites These microscopic mites induce various abnormal growths or galls on the foliage and buds. Their feeding causes abnormally enlarged buds (big bud), or on leaves the excessive growth of hairs (felt galls), raised pimples, or cylindrical structures (nail galls), or thickening and curling of leaf margins.

Cottony cushion scale This sap-sucking pest is found on camellia, holly, rhododendron, *Trachelospermum*, and other evergreen shrubs. Coatings of sooty mold develop

Although galls on foliage and buds may look alarming, gall mites have little impact on plant growth. There is no effective treatment.

Control newly hatched scale nymphs by spraying them with an over-the-counter pesticide.

Caterpillars can sometimes be removed by hand, but for heavy infestations, use an over-the-counter pesticide.

on the insect's excrement on the upper leaf surface. The mature insects are ⅛ in (3–4 mm) long and lay eggs in elongate white waxy bands on the underside of leaves.

Moths Caterpillars of moths, such as buff tip, brown-tail, yellow-tail, and tent caterpillars, eat the foliage of many trees and shrubs. Some, such as leopard moth caterpillars, tunnel in trunks and branches.

Adelgids These small sap-sucking insects are closely related to aphids. They only attack conifers, especially spruce, pine, larch, Douglas fir, and hemlock. The insects are covered in fluffy white wax or concealed inside galls. Small conifers can be sprayed with an appropriately labeled insecticide when adelgids become active in early spring, but they have to be tolerated on large trees.

Nectria canker This disease is caused by the fungus *Nectria cinnabarina* and is commonly seen on dead twigs of trees and shrubs, or in woody debris. It causes problems on plants that are suffering from other stresses. In damp weather, small pink or red cushionlike eruptions are evident on affected bark. The fungus can infect through wounds and, once established, kills branches rapidly. *Magnolia*, *Eleagnus*, *Acer*, figs, currants, and gooseberries are frequently affected.

Adelgids cause little real damage to mature trees, but for smaller ones, see above for treatment suggestions.

To limit entry points for nectria canker infection, carefully prune dead wood. If the problem persists, a wound sealant can help.

Trees, shrubs and climbers: general pest and diseases: *continued*

Witches' broom These are abnormal twig proliferations that are mostly caused by a fungus that can lead to a reduction in flowering. Many trees can be affected, including species of *Abies*, *Betula*, *Prunus*, and *Salix*.

Canker These are dead sections of bark on branches or main trunks of trees. Canker diseases may cause extensive damage to trees when they kill all of the bark in a particular area, thus girdling a branch or main stem. If the trunk is affected, the entire plant may die. Examples of canker diseases are coryneum and phomopsis cankers (confined to *Cupressaceae*), and nectria canker, which mostly damages pears and apples, but can affect other broadleaf trees such as rowan, beech, ash, and holly.

Crown gall This bacterial gall affects many plants, but particularly fruit trees and cane fruits. Plants may struggle, and upon examination a large woody gall is found at ground level or on the roots, caused by soilborne bacteria that injure roots or the stem and cause the abnormal tissue to proliferate. Avoid planting diseased specimens or injuring roots.

Witches' brooms can be cut out of the tree if necessary, although they are only likely to impair flowering potential.

For most cankers, cutting out affected branches below the infected bark retards development. Apply a wound paint to avoid reinfection.

If crown gall is present, grow a crop of potatoes and avoid replanting with a susceptible species.

Removing the fruiting bodies of wood decay fungus does not stop the disease and they usually only appear when infection is well established.

If a plant has tree scabs, destroy fallen leaves or spray with a fungicide labeled for use on this pest on the specific plants it infests.

Wood decay fungi Many different fungi can cause wood decay. Some cause top rots, where airborne spores enter wounds in the canopy and cause branch decay. Others cause root and butt rots, and may be indicated by crown thinning and early leaf loss. Often the first indication of decay will be the appearance of fungal fruiting bodies. Commonly these are brackets, but toadstools and elaborate structures or encrustations are also possible. It is wise to seek professional advice regarding the safety of the tree.

Tree scabs Several trees are affected by scabs caused by fungi. The most significant foliar scab disease is apple and pear scab, which also attacks *Cotoneaster*, rowans, hawthorns, and, less commonly, *Pyracantha*. In addition, there are other fungal species causing scabs on *Pyracantha*, olive, loquat, and willow. Symptoms of tree scabs include dark green patches, which can be seen on the leaves and eventually lead to dead tissues. Dark sunken spots also appear on fruits or berries. Infected leaves then fall prematurely. Recurring infection causes poor growth and dieback of defoliated trees. The disease can be controlled on apples and pears by spraying an appropriately labeled fungicide. The latter can also be used if trees are grown as ornamentals. Varieties resistant to tree scabs are available.

Trees

Several pests and diseases that affect trees are well known to us because of the significance these large plants play in our landscape and heritage.

If you have damage on:
- Acer, see also hydrangea scale (*p.80*) and wisteria scale (*p.85*)
- Hawthorn and *Sorbus*, see pear and cherry slugworm (*p.123*)
- Linden or Eurasian maple, see also horse chestnut scale (*p.72*)

See also:
- General pests and diseases on trees, shrubs, and climbers (*pp.66–69*)
- Know your enemy: pests and diseases (*pp.26–43*)
- Winter moth (*p.110*)

Arbutus leaf spots
Arbutus can be affected by several leaf spot fungi (*see p.40*), including *Septoria unedonis* and *Elsinoë mattirolianum*. The damage by the latter can be severe. The only recommended course of action is to remove the fallen material to reduce infection for the following year and to cut back dying branches to healthy tissue.

Beech woolly aphid
The foliage on beech trees and hedges is infested during late spring and summer by dense colonies of pale yellow aphids covered in fluffy white, waxy secretions. The leaves become sticky with excreted honeydew. Only hedges and small trees can be treated. Spray when aphids are first seen with an approved insecticide.

Acer pimple gall
The foliage of Eurasian maple, field maple, and Japanese acers is affected by this tiny mite. It sucks sap from the lower leaf surface and causes hollow reddish bumps or pimples to grow on the top side of the leaves. During the summer, the mites live and feed inside the pimple galls. No serious damage is caused, so control measures are not required.

Tar spot of *Acer*
It is the fungus *Rhytisma acerinum* that causes tar spot of *Acer*, and the symptoms are large black blotches on the leaves, which are slightly raised and shiny. All the infections in a season arise from spores that have been produced from the previous year's infected overwintered leaves. Tar spot of *Acer* is mainly observed on Eurasian maples, although other maples may be affected. Fortunately, this disease is not very damaging to the tree since its vigor is not often affected. Although there is no chemical control for this particular disease, removing and burning the fallen infected material (*see p.18*), which can drop prematurely, will help to reduce the infection in the following year.

Eucalyptus sucker

Shoot tips and young leaves are infested with the gray or orange flattened nymphs of this sap-sucking insect. Heavily infested shoots may have the tips killed. A grayish-green sooty mold can develop on the insect's sticky excrement. On trees small enough to be sprayed, apply a pesticide registered for use against sucker on eucalyptus trees.

Eucalyptus gall wasp

This tiny black insect lays eggs in eucalyptus leaves in early summer. Small pinkish pustules develop, each containing a single grub. The galls later become grayish-brown. Heavily infested leaves may drop prematurely. On trees small enough to be sprayed, treat with an approved pesticide in early summer. Dispose of fallen leaves before adult gall wasps emerge.

Dutch elm disease

The first signs are browning and yellowing of the leaves. The affected branches die back from the tips and discolored leaves then fall. Symptoms spread until the tree dies. The disease is caused by two fungi and is disseminated by elm bark beetles. Destroy infected trees. There are varieties that are claimed to have good resistance.

Dogwood anthracnose

The symptoms of this fungus are brown spots on the leaves, perhaps with purplish margins surrounded by a yellowish halo. The spot may spread to form a more extensive blotch. Leaves shrivel and small stems may be killed. Defoliation usually starts earlier. Prune out and dispose of infected material. The disease can be devastating, but trees may recover.

Elm gall mite

In late spring, elms develop hard raised swellings on the upper surface of their leaves. These are induced by microscopic gall mites that live and feed within these galls. The mites overwinter underneath the bud scales. No serious damage is caused to the tree, apart from creating the galls. This is fortunate as there are no effective controls.

Trees *continued*

Horse chestnut bleeding canker
Bleeding patches develop on the bark and trees decline. Traditionally this was ascribed to *Phytophthora* (see p.42), but the recent epidemic appears to be caused by a bacterium. Do not cut out infected limbs as this creates new entry points. Unless affected trees are a health hazard, they are best left alone and may recover if they have vigorous crowns.

Horse chestnut leaf blotch
This leaf blotch disease is caused by the fungus *Guignardia aesculi*. As a result of the fungal infection, the leaves develop irregular blotches, which are often outlined by a yellow band, from midsummer onward. The leaves may shrivel and fall prematurely. As the damage occurs late in the season, the health of the tree is usually not affected.

Horse chestnut leaf-mining moth
Tiny caterpillars feed within the leaves, causing elongate white or brown blotch mines. There are at least three generations and by late summer most of the foliage may have turned brown. Control is generally not possible because of the size of the tree. The damage is disfiguring, but the tree won't be killed. *Aesculus indica* is resistant to this pest.

Horse chestnut scale
This sap-sucking insect is most easily seen in early summer when females deposit their eggs on the bark of horse chestnut, linden, and *Acer* species. The eggs are laid under a white waxy substance on which the scale's brown shell is perched. Use an appropriately labeled pesticide on small trees and shrubs to control the newly hatched nymphs.

Lime nail gall mite
During the summer, upright cylindrical structures $\frac{1}{8}$–$\frac{1}{4}$ in (3–5 mm) tall and yellowish-green or red in color grow on the upper leaf surface of linden trees. The hollow galls contain microscopic mites whose feeding activities have induced the galls' growth. No real damage is done and as there is no effective treatment, this gall mite has to be tolerated.

Holm oak leaf miner

There are two species of leaf-mining moths that cause problems on holm oak. The more widespread species causes elongate blotch mines where the caterpillars have eaten out the internal tissues. The other species creates wiggly linear mines. Neither leaf-mining moth can be controlled effectively, so damage has to be tolerated.

Gypsy moth caterpillar

Gypsy moth caterpillars were brought to the United States in the 1860s as a replacement for silkworms. They have become a major pest in eastern and central North America, where they infest oaks and hundreds of other tree species. Each moth lays up to 1,200 eggs that overwinter and hatch in spring. Dense populations of caterpillars eat voraciously throughout the growing season until trees are defoliated. Natural controls include predatory wasps, flies, beetles, spiders, and birds, as well as bacterial and viral diseases. Hard winters and rainy summers reduce numbers. Deter infestation by keeping trees healthy. Treatments include pheromone traps and the bacterial pesticide *Bacillus thuringiensis* (Bt).

Oak gall wasps

More than 30 species of gall wasps occur on common oak. Their larvae cause various abnormal growths, known as galls, on the foliage, buds, catkins, acorns, roots, and stems. Spangle galls and silk button galls (*see above*) occur on the leaves in late summer. None of these gall wasps causes any real damage, so control measures are not required.

Acorn gall wasp

The female gall wasp lays eggs in early summer when oak acorns begin to form. The grubs develop inside the acorns and cause the formation of a ridged woody gall, which entirely or partly replaces the acorn. The gall is fully developed by late summer. Apart from destroying some of an oak tree's seeds, this gall wasp causes no harm. There are no control measures.

Oak powdery mildew

Powdery mildew species that affect oak can be seen as a white, thin, powdery coating sometimes associated with dead patches on the leaves. Premature defoliation occurs, but the vigor of mature trees is rarely affected. Fungicide treatments for oak powdery mildew are not necessary unless the trees are young.

Trees *continued*

Mountain ash gall mite
In late spring, the leaves of rowan or mountain ash develop whitish-green blotches where microscopic mites are feeding inside the leaves. The discolored areas darken until, by midsummer, the leaves have many brown blotches. There is no effective treatment. In years when trees are heavily infested, they can look very unhealthy but will survive.

Walnut gall mite
In summer, walnut leaves develop raised "blisters" on the upper leaf surface. The underside of these blisters is covered in creamy white hairs among which live the microscopic mites. Apart from creating the galls, the mites have no harmful effect on the tree's growth or ability to produce nuts. There are no effective pesticide treatments.

Plane anthracnose
This fungal disease is specific to London plane. The spores require wet conditions in which to germinate, and are also splashed around in rain droplets. Symptoms vary and include premature leaf fall, twig dieback, and browning on either side of the main leaf vein. Vigor of trees is not usually affected. No fungicide treatment is available, nor is it necessary.

Quince leaf blight
Irregular brown spots develop on the leaves of quince and other plants in the rose family, which blacken and fall prematurely. Shoots or fruits can be attacked. Infections proliferate in the summer and the fungus overwinters on shoots. Infected tissues and fallen leaves should be disposed of. The variety 'Krymsk' is supposedly resistant to the disease.

Robinia decline
Since 2007, *Robinia* 'Frisia' has been declining. Branches die back and the tree ultimately dies. Several factors thought to contribute to this include unusually wet summers, a leaf-spot fungus, and root diseases such as honey fungus and *Phytophthora* (*see pp.42–43*) and *Phomopsis* dieback. Prune affected trees to help limit the spread of *Phomopsis*.

Poplar canker

The bacterium *Xanthomonas populi* infects through wounds and natural openings. It overwinters in bark cankers and in spring, bacteria ooze out of bark cracks and spread by wind or rain splash. It causes dieback on young branches. On large branches and stems, large cankers may develop. Cut out infected parts when symptoms first appear.

Willow leaf beetle

The foliage of willows and poplar develop brown, dried-up patches where the ⅛-in- (3–4-mm-) long, metallic bronzy-green adult beetles and their black larvae have grazed away the leaf surface. By late summer, the foliage may have been extensively damaged. On small trees, spray with an approved pesticide when damage is seen.

Giant willow aphid

Dense colonies of a large grayish-black aphid occur on the bark of willow branches and trunks in late summer. They excrete a sticky honeydew that often attracts wasps. Little real damage is done to the tree, but the stickiness and wasps can be a nuisance. If necessary, small willows can be sprayed with pyrethrum, following label directions.

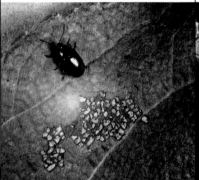
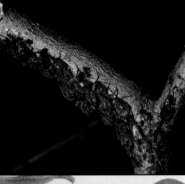

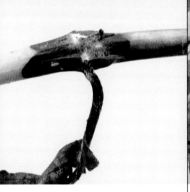

Willow bean gall sawfly

Hard red or yellowish-green bean-shaped swellings, about ¼ in (6 mm) long, develop in willow leaves in early and late summer. Each gall contains a caterpillar-like larva that gradually hollows out the gall. Damage is confined to the creation of the galls and the tree's health and vigor are unimpaired. Control measures are therefore not required.

Willow black canker

Black canker is caused by a fungus that infects older twigs and smaller branches and overwinters in lesions on the stems. Infections first cause irregular black spots on the leaves, which spread to the stems. The disease is prevalent in cool, wet weather when new foliage appears. Some varieties are more resistant. This disease must be tolerated.

Willow anthracnose

Small brown spots caused by a fungus appear on leaves, leading to early defoliation, and black cankers form on stems, causing dieback. In damp seasons, willow anthracnose can be extremely damaging. Trees will recover in drier years, however, and the disease must be tolerated. *Salix* x *sepulcralis* var. *chrysocoma* is the worst affected.

Conifers and hedges

A sick hedge or conifer can be a constant source of irritation for a gardener if the desired effect is for a uniform color or shape.

If you have damage on:
- Juniper, see pear rust (*p.123*)
- Privet, see lilac leaf miner (*p.78*) in addition to privet thrips (*below*)
- Silver fir, see fuchsia rust (*p.79*)

See also:
- General pests and diseases on trees, shrubs, and climbers (*pp.66–69*)
- Know your enemy: pests and diseases (*pp.26–43*)

Green spruce aphid
This small, dark green aphid is active from fall to spring on *Picea* species, especially Norway spruce. The foliage becomes mottled and drops in late winter or spring. New growth is in sharp contrast to the damaged foliage. Spray with dormant oil or an appropriately labeled insecticide. Damaged trees will take several years to recover.

Conifer red spider mite
Tiny yellowish-green mites suck sap from the foliage of conifers, especially spruce. This causes a fine mottling of the foliage, which gradually becomes yellowish-brown as the summer progresses. It is mainly a problem on small conifers in sunny locations. If necessary, spray with an approved pesticide, or hose plants with water daily, in the morning.

Cypress aphid
This aphid is a common cause of extensive dieback on *Cupressus*, *Chamaecyparis* and Leyland cypress hedges in late summer. Lower parts are worst affected. Black sooty molds, which grow on aphid excrement, may be seen on infested stems. Spray in late spring with dormant oil or an insecticide labeled for use against this pest on evergreens.

Privet thrips
The foliage on privet hedges and lilac becomes silvery brown in late summer as a result of thrips sucking sap from the leaves. The adult thrips have narrow, elongate bodies, 1/12 in (2 mm) long, and are blackish-brown with white bands across the wings. The nymphs are yellowish-white. If necessary, spray with a pesticide approved for this purpose.

Holly leaf miner
Most hollies, especially clipped hedges, have some leaf miner damage, developing between early summer and spring. The maggots of a tiny fly feed inside the leaves, causing yellowish-purple blotch mines. Although unsightly, the damage is small. Due to the thick waxy surface of holly leaves, sprays are ineffective against the leaf miner.

Holly leaf blight

Symptoms are circular black spots on the leaves, which fall rapidly. *Phytophthora itius* also infects young stems, leading to black lesions. In hedges, infections spread to form "arches" of defoliation. There are no fungicides available to amateur gardeners, so control depends on ensuring that no infected plants are brought into the garden.

Escallonia leaf spots

There are two new leaf spots that are very damaging on escallonia foliage. They cause brown/purple spots on the leaves and then defoliation and stem dieback.Cut back infected branches to healthy tissue and remove fallen material to reduce disease spread. Mulch the ground at the base of the plant to prevent infected soil from splashing onto it.

Cedar leaf blight

The leaf blight fungus *Didymascella thujina* (syn. *Keithia thujina*) is specific to *Thuja*, usually a problem seen more in nurseries as it affects and can kill plants that are less than four years old. Susceptibility lessens with age. The fungus can be seen as black bodies on the dead leaves, later falling out to leave cavities. No control is necessary on planted trees.

Yew Phytophthora root rot

Yew is extremely susceptible to the root rot pathogen *Phytophthora*. Affected plants show bronze foliage and infection of fine roots causes the roots to snap, resulting in black discoloration of the root tips and a reduced root system. Remove affected plants, improve drainage, and keep the area free of woody plants for at least three years.

Laurel diseases

Leaves of laurel are often affected by powdery mildew, leaf spot fungi, and bacterial shothole, all of which can cause holes, tattering, and distortion in the leaves. Application of a general fertilizer and foliar fertilizer helps to boost the vigor of the tree. Suitably labeled fungicides may be used to control fungal problems.

Pestalotiopsis

In the last decade, *Pestalotiopsis* has been increasingly reported to cause widespread damage to a number of plants, including many conifers. The symptoms are browning followed by death of the foliage. The only option is the removal of the dead and dying foliage. Minimize further infection by ensuring that any healthy plants are kept in good condition.

Shrubs

The smaller size of shrubs means that problems are more apparent, being at eye level. It also means treatment of the whole plant is more feasible.

If you have damage on:
- Buddleia, see figwort weevil (*p.79*) and mullein moth (*p.92*)
- *Chaenomeles* and *Sorbus*, see pear and cherry slugworm (*p.123*)
- *Mahonia*, see mahonia rust (*p.81*) and berberis sawfly (*right*)
- *Phygelius*, see figwort weevil (*p.79*)

See also:
- General pests and diseases on trees, shrubs, and climbers (*pp.66–69*)

Berberis sawfly
Whitish green caterpillar-like larvae with black spots and yellow blotches defoliate some deciduous *Berberis*, especially *B. thunbergii*, and *Mahonia*. There are two or three generations between late spring and early fall. When fully fed, the larvae go into the soil to pupate. Spray the young larvae with pyrethrum, carefully following the package directions.

Broom gall mite
Whitish-green cauliflower-like enlarged buds develop on the stems of broom (*Cytisus*) during the summer. These galls contain microscopic mites whose feeding has induced the abnormal growth. Later, the galls become grayish-brown and dry up. There is no effective chemical treatment. Pick off the galled buds or destroy heavily infested plants.

Gleditsia gall midge
From late spring onward, gleditsia leaves fail to develop normally. The leaflets form small pods that contain several whitish-orange maggots. Several generations occur over the summer months, with the degree of galling progressively building up. The leaf galls dry up and drop off, creating bare branch tips in late summer. There is no effective control.

Laburnum leaf miner
Laburnum foliage is mined by fly and moth larvae. Caterpillars of the latter create roughly circular, whitish-brown mines up to ½ in (10 mm) in diameter. Maggots of the leaf-mining fly make irregular blotch mines along the leaf margins. Neither cause serious harm, as heavy infestations do not usually occur before late summer. There is no effective control.

Lilac leaf miner
Lilac and privet foliage develops large brown blotch mines in early and late summer where the caterpillars have eaten the internal tissues. When half grown, the caterpillars emerge and complete their feeding inside the rolled leaf tip, which is held in place with silk threads. Remove affected leaves on lilac or clip infested privet hedges to reduce the infestation.

Cotoneaster webber moth
Two moths with small dark brown caterpillars attack *Cotoneaster horizontalis*. Hawthorn webber moth caterpillars cover their feeding area with sheets of white silk. Porphyry knothorn caterpillars live in silk tubes spun along the stems. Both cause brown foliage, mainly in early summer. Spray caterpillars with an approved pesticide or prune out infested shoots.

Pyracantha leaf miner
The foliage develops distinctive oval-shaped silvery white mines in the center of the upper leaf surface where the caterpillar is feeding inside the leaf. The heaviest infestations are often in mid–late winter, but mined leaves can be found at other times of year. Little real damage is done, even when plants are heavily infested, so control measures are not required.

Figwort weevil
Several species of figwort weevils occur on figwort, buddleia, mullein, and *Phygelius*. The adults are $1/12$–$1/8$ in (2–4 mm) long and grayish-white with a circular black spot on the wing cases. The larvae are slimy, yellowish brown grubs which, like the adults, eat the foliage and flower buds. Spray the pests with a product labeled for this purpose.

Elephant hawk moth on fuchsia
Fully grown caterpillars are about 3 in (80 mm) long and have two pairs of eyelike markings at the head end. Mature caterpillars are mainly blackish brown, but are sometimes green. They eat the foliage of many plants, but in gardens they feed mainly on fuchsia. Infestations usually consist of one or two caterpillars, so hand removal is feasible.

Fuchsia rust
It is the fungus *Pucciniastrum epilobii* that causes fuchsia rust. It also infects willow herbs (*Epilobium*) and alternates between those and silver firs (*Abies*). Yellow spots appear on the upper leaf surfaces, corresponding to orange pustules on the lower surfaces, leading to death of leaves. Black overwintering spores have only been found on willow herbs.

The fungal spores on willow herbs germinate in the spring and subsequently infect species of silver fir. Likewise, spores produced on firs can then infect fuchsias, although the disease may be present on fuchsia year-round. Fuchsias are sensitive to spray damage, so check the label of fungicides labeled for rust carefully before applying.

Shrubs *continued*

Pieris lacebug
A coarse pale mottling develops on the upper leaf surface of pieris and rhododendron leaves. Adult pieris lacebugs are ⅛ in (3 mm) long and have transparent wings with black markings. Both adults and the spiny blackish-brown nymphs live on the underside of the leaves from late spring to fall. Spray them with an a pesticide approved for this use.

Hydrangea scale
The stems and undersides of leaves of hydrangea, *Acer*, and *Prunus* are covered with white, waxy, oval-shaped egg masses about ⅛ in (4 mm) long in early summer. This pest sucks sap from the foliage in the summer, and heavy infestations weaken plants. Control by spraying the nymphs with an appropriately labeled pesticide in midsummer.

Euonymus scale
Mainly found on the leaves and stems of *Euonymus japonicus*, where these insects suck sap. The tiny male scales have elongate white shells; females have blackish-brown, pear-shaped coverings. Infested foliage develops a yellowish mottling, followed by leaf drop. Spray with an approved pesticide in midsummer and early fall to control the young nymphs.

Boxwood sucker
Damage is caused in late spring by the pale green, flattened immature nymphs of this sap-sucking insect. They stunt the new shoots and distort the leaves, giving shoot tips a cabbagelike appearance. This pest is not a problem for boxwood that is clipped to restrict growth. Spray young plants when new shoots emerge with an approved pesticide.

Boxwood blight
There are two fungi that can cause boxwood leaves to turn brown, followed by defoliation and dieback. *Cylindrocladium buxicola* causes black streaks on stems. *Volutella buxi* needs wounds or stressed plants to infect, but once it has taken hold in the main stem, the plant may die. *C. buxicola* is very damaging and difficult to control once present, so keep new plants separate from existing ones for a month to ensure they are clean. All boxwood species are susceptible, but tightly clipped dwarf varieties are worst affected. To prevent boxwood blight from spreading further, destroy affected plants and fallen leaves and replace the topsoil. Fungicides labeled for use on ornamentals have limited success for both diseases.

Viburnum beetle

Only *Viburnum tinus* and *V. opulus* are extensively defoliated by creamy white, black-marked beetle larvae, up to ⅜ in (9 mm) long, in mid- to late spring. Some further damage is caused by the grayish-brown adult beetles in late summer. Look for holes in the new growth in April and then spray with a pesticide labeled for this purpose.

Viburnum whitefly

Viburnum tinus is attacked by this sap-sucking insect. The white-winged adults occur in summer and are 1⁄12 in (2 mm) long. It is the overwintering, black oval nymphs encrusted with white wax on the underside of leaves that are most often seen. Control is not usually required, but if necessary, spray in midsummer with a suitably labeled insecticide.

Hebe downy mildew

Peronospora grisea can be seen underneath the leaves as a grayish fungus corresponding to yellow patches on the upper surfaces. The plants may subsequently be defoliated and growth of plants checked. No chemical control is available for hebe downy mildew, so all you can do is destroy infected leaves or plants.

Mahonia rust

The symptoms of mahonia rust are orange or red purple spots on the top of leaves corresponding with dark brown spots on the underside. Heavy infections cause premature leaf drop. The disease enjoys humid air, so prune out the affected branches to improve ventilation and destroy fallen leaves. If necessary, spray with an approved fungicide for rusts.

Yucca leaf spot

The symptoms for this leaf spot are yellowish and brown lesions. They are generally elliptical and are seen scattered across the upper surface of the leaves. There are no fungicides available to control fungal leaf spots. Remove the infected leaves and avoid overhead watering, or protect the plant from rainfall.

Azaleas, camellias, and rhododendrons

Fortunately, camellias and rhododendrons are not often affected by pests and diseases, and those that do arise are mostly treatable.

See also:
- General pests and diseases on trees, shrubs, and climbers (*pp.66–69*)
- Know your enemy: pests and diseases (*pp.26–43*)
- Pieris lacebug (*p.80*), powdery mildew (*p.40*), and *Phytophthora* (p.42), which can also affect rhododendrons

Azalea and camellia galls
Azalea gall causes dramatic swellings on the leaves of plants. The green galls become covered in a white spore bloom, which will spread the infection. Remove the galls by hand before they turn white. A similar fungus causes large round or forked galls on camellias that also develop a white bloom. Plant vigor is not affected. Prune out promptly.

Camellia petal blight
Caused by *Ciborinia camelliae*, camellia petal blight begins with small brown flecks on the petals that eventually spread over whole flowers. The flowers then fall early. It can be confused with frost damage, but if affected by the disease, a white or gray fungus can be seen under the petals when they are separated from the calyx. Dispose of affected flowers, as there are no chemicals available. If you don't, the fungus forms a black structure at the base of the petals, which remains dormant until the next flowering season, when it germinates to produce a fruiting body. This will release spores that are wind-dispersed to land on petals, continuing the cycle. A deep mulch might also help to break the cycle.

Camellia yellow mottle virus
Camellia yellow mottle virus causes bright yellow or creamy-white blotches or speckling on the dark green leaves. The virus may also cause flower breaking. The vigor of the plant is not affected, but prune out affected branches and do not propagate to help prevent the virus from spreading. The vector for camellia yellow mottle is unknown.

Rhododendron leafhopper

Adult leafhoppers, which are ³/₈ in (8 mm) long and turquoise green with red stripes, occur in late summer. The females lay overwintering eggs in next year's flower buds, creating infection sites for bud blast disease (*see below*). Remove dead buds as they develop and spray the plant in late summer with a suitably labeled pesticide to reduce egg laying.

Rhododendron leaf spots

The fungus *Glomerella cingulata* causes irregular purple brown spots. If only a few leaves are diseased, dispose of them together with any leaves showing brown patches. A systemic fungicide applied for powdery mildew may control this disease. Encourage vigor in affected shrubs by good cultivation, including the use of a foliar fertilizer.

Rhododendron leaf blight

Several *Phytophthora* species, including *P. ramorum*, can cause leaf blight and twig dieback. Brown, spreading lesions develop on leaves, sometimes with a V-shaped appearance, followed by wilting and dieback. Cut back infected shoots to healthy tissues. If you suspect *P. ramorum*, do not propagate the affected plants.

Rhododendron rust

The upper leaf surfaces develop yellowish patches and, in the summer, fungal pustules containing orange and brown spores develop on the undersides. The fungus lives within affected leaves, so they are infected until they fall. The disease, therefore, appears every season. Dispose of affected leaves and spray with an approved fungicide for rusts.

Rhododendron bud blast

Bud blast kills flower buds on rhododendrons, leading to a reduction in flowers. The buds become covered in black, pinhead-like structures. This fungus (*Pycnostysanus azaleae*) is spread by the rhododendron leafhopper (*see above*), and control of the insect may reduce new infections. Pick off dead buds when they are seen.

Rhododendron powdery mildew

Powdery mildew can appear in winter or spring and discolors leaves. A faint fungal growth on the lower surface corresponds with red or yellow blotches on the upper leaf. Ensuring that the plant has plenty of water and spraying it with products that are effective against powdery mildew will help.

Climbers

When a well-loved climber begins to ail, or a newly planted specimen unexpectedly dies, the first reaction is often one of bafflement. Establishing the cause is not always easy, but here are some common culprits.

See also:
- General pests and diseases on trees, shrubs, and climbers (*pp.66–69*)
- Know your enemy: pests and diseases (*pp.26–43*)

Earwig on clematis
Earwigs (*see p.31*) hide away during the day in dark crevices and then emerge at night, when they eat the petals and young foliage of clematis and many other plants. They are active from spring to fall. Earwigs can be trapped in flower pots loosely stuffed with dry grass, or spray plants at dusk with an insecticide labeled for this use.

Clematis slime flux
Affected clematis shoots become covered with a foul-smelling cream, pink, or orange slimy growth. The original cause of most slime fluxes is a wound through which some of the plant's sap escapes. The stem often dies above this point. There are no chemical controls and it is best to cut back the stem below this wound, removing the diseased tissue.

Clematis wilt
Clematis wilt is caused by the fungus *Phoma clematidina*. Leaves and shoots of clematis wilt and die rapidly, although recovery is possible from healthy tissue either below soil level or from nodes that are beneath the wilted area. The wilt usually starts at the tips of the shoots, followed by blackening of the leaf stalks leading to wilting. Affected growth should be cut back to clean tissue, even if this is below ground level. Plant clematis in deep and fertile soil in a moist and shaded area to encourage good root growth, which will subsequently help combat wilt. Large-flowered hybrids are most susceptible to clematis wilt. Clematis species, including *C. montana*, are resistant and *C. viticella* is tolerant of infection.

Ivy leaf spot
Various fungi cause brown or gray spots on ivy foliage and, on variegated leaves, leaf spot is usually at its most acute on the white or pale areas. It doesn't usually affect the plant's vigor. Clip severely affected branches to help prevent the leaf spot from spreading, and, if possible, spray with fungicides that are labeled for this use.

Honeysuckle aphid

Dense colonies of grayish-green aphids develop on the shoot tips and flower buds in late spring to early summer. Flower buds may be killed and the foliage is discolored and distorted. A sticky honeydew is excreted by the aphids and this allows sooty molds to grow. Spray the aphids with pyrethrum or another insecticide labeled for this use.

Honeysuckle powdery mildew

Typically, a powdery white coating appears on the leaves, infected tissue becomes distorted, and leaves may drop. Outbreaks are most severe in dry soil conditions, so water regularly and also remove infected tissues to reduce further spread. Encourage air circulation by pruning. Spraying with an appropriately labeled fungicide may also help.

Wisteria dieback

While a soilborne disease such as honey fungus, *Phytophthora* root rot or *Verticillium* wilt (*see pp.42–43*) can be responsible for dieback, sudden wilting may, in fact, be because wisterias are grafted near ground level and graft failure may occur after many years. If this is the case, a new wisteria can be planted in the same position.

Wisteria scale

This is an unusually large blackish-brown scale, measuring up to ½ in (10 mm) in diameter. It sucks sap from the stems of wisteria, *Prunus*, and *Acer* species, sometimes causing dieback. On plants small enough to be sprayed, apply an approved pesticide in early summer, making sure to follow the package directions carefully.

Passion flower viruses

Passiflora can show typical symptoms of viruses. These include leaf distortion, yellowing, and leaf mottling. When grown indoors, they may be infected by common viruses occurring in greenhouses (*see p.139*). There are no cures and it is best to destroy plants showing symptoms if these persist. Sterilize tools and wash hands when handling infected plants.

Roses

Pests and diseases are the bane of rose growers, from greenfly infestations to black spot. Good cultivation and hygiene can reduce some problems, and most modern roses have been bred for their resistance to disease.

See also:
- General pests and diseases on trees, shrubs, and climbers (*pp.66–69*)
- Know your enemy: pests and diseases (*pp.26–43*), most specifically leaf-cutting bees (*p.31*), downy and powdery mildews (*p.40*), and honey fungus (*p.43*), which roses are especially likely to suffer from.

Large rose sawfly larvae
The yellow-and-black females insert eggs into soft young rose stems in early and late summer. The pale green larvae are marked with black spots and yellow blotches. They feed ravenously and can rapidly defoliate the stems before going down into the soil to pupate. Remove the larvae by hand or spray with a pesticide labeled for control of this pest on roses.

Rose aphid
Several species of greenfly or aphids suck sap from the foliage, shoot tips, and flower buds during the spring and summer. Heavy infestations cause stunted growth and poor flowering. White aphid skins, honeydew, and sooty mold disfigure the plants. Spray infestations early with a pesticide labeled for use against this pest on roses.

Rose leaf-rolling sawfly
The small black females lay eggs in rose leaflets, causing them to curl downward and form leaf rolls. After hatching, the pale green caterpillar-like larva eats the rolled leaf. There is one generation in late spring to early summer. Remove rolled leaflets to prevent larvae from completing their feeding. Spraying with an approved pesticide may give some control.

Rose slugworm sawfly
The pale green, semitransparent caterpillar-like larvae, up to ⅝ in (15 mm) long, graze away the lower leaf surface, causing the damaged area to dry up and become whitish-brown. There are two generations, with damage occurring in early and late summer. If necessary, control by spraying with a pesticide labeled for this purpose.

Robin's pincushion
Hard swellings, up to the size of a golf ball, develop in late summer on the stems of wild roses, sucker growth, and some garden species roses. These galls are covered in mosslike reddish-yellow modified leaves. The gall is induced by small white grubs that develop inside the structure. No real damage is caused, so control is unnecessary.

Rose leafhopper

A coarse pale mottling develops on the upper leaf surface where the insect sucks sap from the underside of leaves, especially on roses in sheltered places. Adult rose leafhoppers are pale yellow and ⅛ in (3 mm) long and jump off the plant when disturbed. If a damaging infestation is developing, control with pyrethrum, following package directions carefully.

Rose black spot

Dark brown or black blotches appear on leaves from late spring onward and affected leaves fall prematurely, which can weaken the plant. Encouraging vigorous growth will help plants. Initial infection is mainly from spots on stems in which the fungus *Diplocarpon rosae* has overwintered. Severe spring pruning to remove this tissue helps, as does thorough leaf clearance in fall and mulching in spring. Various fungicides are available to help kill the fungus, and alternating applications of different active ingredients will help to identify the most effective product. First spray immediately after spring pruning, and then spray once again when the leaves open.

Rose canker and dieback

Various fungi can cause canker and dieback of rose stems. Most infect the plant through bad pruning cuts or wounds. It is also important to plant roses so their graft union is not covered by soil and make clean pruning cuts close above a bud. To discourage dieback, feed with commercial rose fertilizers and avoid drought or waterlogging.

Rose viruses

Several viruses are recorded on roses causing vein clearing, yellow flecking, or mottling on the leaves. The markings may be mild and not as clear as on other plants, but leaves may also be distorted and plants stunted as a result of the viral infection. No cures are available for viruses, and it is best to destroy plants (*see also p.41*).

Rose rust

In spring, elongate patches of rust appear on stems and leaf stalks, followed by small bright orange dusty spots on the undersides of leaves, which turn brown by late summer. Often, plants suffer severe defoliation. The spores overwinter on plant debris, soil, and stems. Cut out lesions on stems and destroy fallen leaves. Fungicides are available.

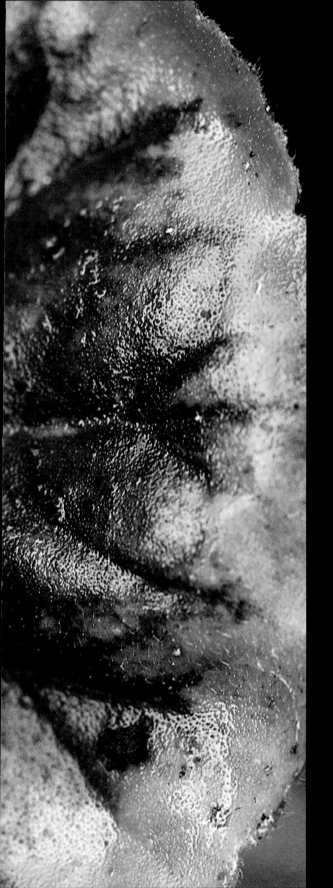

The herbaceous garden

Flower beds provide color in the yard from spring to fall. Even when most of the annuals, bulbs, and perennial herbaceous plants have died down at the end of the growing season, some still have foliage and seed heads to provide interest into fall and beyond. Most yards also have a lawn, and this expanse of mown grass between the beds needs to be kept in a healthy state if it is to provide a pleasing effect that enhances the floral display. Regular inspections will keep plants at their best by allowing early detection of problems and their timely treatment.

Herbaceous plants: general pests and diseases

Herbaceous perennial plants, bulbs, and annuals can suffer from a wide range of pests and diseases, some of which can kill or seriously disfigure the plants.

Inspect plants at regular intervals so that signs of poor health or pest activity are detected in time for appropriate treatment.

The plant divisions in this chapter are:
- Perennials (*see pp.92–97*)
- Annuals (*see pp.98–99*)
- Bulbs, corms, tubers, and rhizomes (*see pp.100–103*)
- Lawns (*see pp.104–105*)

Swift moth caterpillars These live in the soil and feed on roots. They have brown heads and slender white bodies up to 2 in (50 mm) long, with three pairs of short legs at the head end and five pairs of clasper legs on the abdomen.

Tortrix moth caterpillars Pale green and up to ¾ in (18 mm) long, tortrix moth caterpillars bind two leaves together with silk threads and graze away the inner surfaces. Damaged areas dry up and turn brown. Many herbaceous plants and shrubs are attacked.

There is no effective insecticide control for swift moth caterpillars, but a pathogenic nematode is available from biocontrol suppliers.

The hidden nature of tortrix moth caterpillars makes control difficult with sprays. One nonchemical control is to squeeze the bound-up leaves to crush the caterpillars. As well as attacking plants in the garden, they are a problem in greenhouses (*see p.138*).

Green stink bug Both the all-green, shield-shaped adult bugs and their spotted nymphs feed on the sap of beans, peas, tomatoes, raspberries, and many ornamental plants in late summer. The adults grow to ⅝ in (15 mm) long.

Leaf and bud eelworms These microscopic wormlike nematodes live inside the foliage of penstemon, Japanese anemones, chrysanthemums, and many other plants. They cause blackish-brown discolored areas in the leaves, which are often sharply divided from uninfested parts by the larger leaf veins. Damage is mainly seen in late summer to fall.

Powdery mildew This fungus infects many herbaceous plants, and the main ones that are affected are covered in the relevant groups on the following pages. Symptoms include a powdery white coating appearing on any part of the plant and infected tissue becoming distorted. If it takes hold, subsequently the leaves may drop, buds die, or stems die back.

If necessary, green stink bugs can be controlled by spraying them with pyrethrum or an approved pesticide.

There is no chemical control for leaf and bud eelworms. Dig out heavily infested plants.

Thin out shoots to improve air circulation, which helps reduce the incidence of disease. Fungicide sprays will also help.

Perennials

On perennials, pests and diseases may come and go, or they may be a persistent problem, such as hollyhock rust.

If you have damage on:
- Auriculas, see root aphid (*p.33*)
- Cineraria, gerbera, or oxeye daisies, see chrysanthemum leaf miner (*p.95*)
- Freesias or gladioli, see canna viruses (*p.97*)
- Lavatera, see hollyhock rust (*p.97*)
- Verbascum, see figwort weevil (*p.79*) as well as mullein moth (*below*)

See also:
- General pests and diseases on herbaceous plants (*pp.90–91*)
- Know your enemy: pests and diseases (*pp.26–43*)

Phlox eelworm
The microscopic wormlike eelworms or nematodes live inside the stems and foliage. Infested plants are stunted, with abnormally swollen stems and foliage at the shoot tips, greatly reduced in width. Such stems often rot off. There is no chemical treatment, so destroy infested plants. Put replacement plants in a different part of the garden.

Phormium mealybug
This grayish-white sap-sucking insect lives in the folded bases of the leaves on New Zealand flax. It secretes a white waxy powder from its body. Heavily infested plants lack vigor and suffer dieback. There is no treatment because of difficulties in reaching the pest with an insecticide. Inspect new plants carefully to be sure you are not also buying the pest.

Sempervivum leaf miner
Sempervivums are damaged by the larvae of a leaf-mining hoverfly. Two generations occur in early and late summer, when the larvae hollow out the leaves in the outer portion of the rosettes, causing them to rot or dry up. Remove infested leaves as they appear, or treat container plants with a systemic insecticide labeled for use against this problem.

Mullein moth
The caterpillars are up to 1¾ in (48 mm) long and grayish-white with black spots and yellow blotches. They eat the foliage and flowers of verbascums and sometimes buddleia in summer. When they complete their feeding, they go into the soil to pupate. Remove the caterpillars by hand or spray with pyrethrum or a pesticide labeled for use on this pest.

Solomon's seal sawfly
Grayish-white caterpillar-like larvae, up to 1 in (25 mm) long, devour the foliage on Solomon's seal in early summer. Plants can be reduced to bare stems. There is one generation a year and the fully fed larvae go into the soil to overwinter. Look for holes in the foliage and pick off the larvae, or spray with pyrethrum or a pesticide labeled for use on this pest.

Water lily beetle

Both the grayish brown beetles and their black grubs are up to ³/₈ in (8 mm) long. They live on the upper surface of water lily leaves, where they eat out elongate slots. This damage encourages rotting and discoloration of the leaves. Insecticides cannot be used because of the danger to fish and other pond life, so remove the beetles and larvae by hand if possible.

Water lily aphid

In summer, the upper surface of water lily leaves and the flower buds can be covered with brownish green aphids that are about ¹/₁₂ in (2 mm) long and their white cast skins. If the infestation is great, plant growth and flowering can be poor. Other floating pond plants may also be attacked. The aphids overwinter as eggs on plums and cherries, feeding on their young foliage before moving to water lilies in early summer. In late summer, the aphids migrate back to their winter host plants to lay eggs. Insecticides cannot be used against this pest because all pesticides are dangerous to fish and other pond wildlife. Instead, wipe aphids off the foliage and flower buds, or use a strong jet of water to blast them off.

Violet gall midge

Several generations of this tiny fly lay eggs on the developing leaves of violets during the spring and summer. Infested leaves fail to unfurl and are greatly swollen, and orange-white maggots develop under the curled leaf margins. Plants generally survive this pest and still produce growth and flowers. This is fortunate, as there is no effective control.

New York aster mite

It is mainly *Aster novi-belgii* that is affected by these microscopic mites, which live in the shoot tips and flower buds, where they suck sap. This causes stunted growth with scarring on the stems. Flowers are converted into rosettes of small leaves with no petals. There is no treatment. so dispose of infested plants. *Aster novae-angliae* and *A. amellus* are not damaged.

Geum sawfly

Pale green larvae, up to ⁵/₈ in (15 mm) long and with forked spines on their upper surface, devour the young leaves of geums in late spring to early summer. Leaves can be stripped to the central veins. Remove caterpillars by hand or spray with pyrethrum or an insecticide labeled for this pest. If plants are in flower, use insecticides in the evening to avoid harming bees.

Perennials *continued*

Geranium sawfly

From late spring to the end of summer, the foliage of cranesbills develops holes made by the caterpillar-like sawfly larvae. They are grayish-green with black heads and are up to ½ in (11 mm) long. Two or three generations occur over the summer. Only control if the leaves are being severely holed. Spray with pyrethrum, following label directions.

Geranium powdery mildew

Symptoms of white powdery coating are seen on both the upper and lower surfaces of cranesbill leaves, which are caused by several species of fungi. Improving air circulation by pruning and making sure the roots are kept moist by watering during dry periods, together with mulching in the spring, will go some way toward reducing the infection.

Pelargonium rust

This rust causes yellow blotches on geranium leaves, corresponding to a ring of brown pustules on the lower surfaces. In severe attacks, both surfaces may be infected. Leaves turn yellow and fall, weakening the plant so much that it may die. Destroy badly infected leaves or plants. Improve ventilation, and spray with fungicide labeled for control of rusts.

Lupine aphid

Grayish-white aphids, up to ⅛ in (4 mm) long, form dense colonies on the underside of lupine leaves and on the flower spikes. Plants become sticky with honeydew excreted by the pest. In heavy attacks, the plant may wilt and die. Check lupines for signs of infestation during the spring and, if necessary, spray with pyrethrum, following package directions.

Lupine anthracnose

This is a serious fungal disease of lupines. Large lesions develop on the stems or leaves, which can then lead to rapid collapse. Sometimes pink spores are also evident within the diseased tissue. Affected plants should be removed and destroyed. The fungus can be seedborne. No fungicide is currently available to control this disease.

Hemerocallis gall midge

Eggs are laid on daylily buds during late spring to early summer. Many tiny maggots feed inside the buds, making them abnormally swollen and squat, and they dry up or rot without opening. There are no insecticide treatments, so destroy galled buds before the larvae complete their feeding. Cultivars flowering after mid-July escape damage.

Chrysanthemum leaf miner
This tiny fly has larvae that make narrow, twisting white or brown tunnels (or mines) in the foliage of chrysanthemums, cineraria, gerbera, oxeye daisy, and other related plants. Several generations a year occur on indoor plants. For light infestations, picking off affected parts of leaves, or spraying with pyrethrum according to label directions, may control the larvae.

Chrysanthemum white rust
White rust is a relatively new disease, but is now more widespread than brown rust (*right*). It has dirty white pustules on the lower leaf surface with corresponding pale craters on the upper leaf. Destroy affected plants and neighboring chrysanthemums and do not propagate from them. Spray with a fungicide for control of rusts on ornamentals.

Chrysanthemum brown rust
Brown rust appears in late summer, although many cultivars are now resistant. Dark brown pustules on the underside of leaves correspond with pale green spots on the upper surface. It can cause defoliation and a reduction in flowering. Destroy diseased material and strip lower leaves from cuttings when taken and transplanted. Use fungicides for control of rusts.

Delphinium bacterial leaf spot
This bacterial disease starts on delphinium leaves, but then spreads to the plant's stems and flowers. The bacteria are splashed from the soil and infect through the leaves to cause large black blotches. No chemicals are labeled to control this disease, so all that remains is to destroy badly affected plants as soon as possible.

Delphinium powdery mildew
Delphiniums are particularly prone to powdery mildew, especially in hot summers. The symptoms are a white powdery coating on the leaves and stems. To help control, avoid overcrowding, destroy infected plant material, and spray with an appropriate fungicide. Delphinium Pacific Hybrids Series might be resistant to this disease.

Dianthus smut
The symptoms of dianthus smut are stunting of the flower stalks and distortion of the anthers, which are filled with spores of the fungus *Microbotryum dianthorum*. The fungus probably occurs throughout the plant, so do not take cuttings, and destroy the affected plants before the buds open. Rest the soil for at least five years before replanting.

Perennials *continued*

Peony gray mold

A common fungal disease of peonies is caused by the fungus *Botrytis paeoniae*. In spring or early summer, shoots may wilt and die. A gray, fluffy mold can be seen on brown areas at the stem base, and brown blotches appear on leaves, particularly at their tips. The fungus produces airborne spores and sclerotia, which can remain dormant in the soil, so it is important to promptly cut back affected tissue, if necessary to below soil level. This material should not be composted and the soil around the crown of the plant needs to be replaced. The disease thrives in humid conditions, so peony clumps must not become too dense. No fungicides are currently available that will control this disease.

Acanthus powdery mildew

White powdery coating is seen on the upper surfaces of the leaves. Once established, acanthus can become very densely planted, so to help prevent the disease, thin out the plants as much as possible, cut out infected material, and only water around the roots. Spraying with a fungicide labeled for this purpose may help.

Hellebore black death

Black death is a viral disease that causes the blackening and severe distortion of hellebore leaves and flowers. In early stages, black streaks are evident in leaf and sepal veins. It cannot be eradicated and is not well understood. Dig up affected plants and burn them. Spray neighboring hellebores with an insecticide labeled for aphids to reduce virus spread.

Hellebore leaf blotch

Hellebore leaf spot is caused by the fungus *Microsphaeropsis hellebori*. Large brown spots appear on the leaves, which eventually become silvery. In severe cases, the whole leaf may die, weakening the remaining plant. Sometimes flower stems and the hellebore flowers may be affected, resulting in drooping stems. Infection can occur very rapidly under appropriate damp conditions. Removal of the previous year's foliage before the emergence of flowers will reduce the inoculum that overwinters. Even if you end up removing a lot of the leaves from the hellebore plant, they should soon regenerate. Destroy affected material promptly. A fungicide labeled for this problem may give some control.

Hollyhock rust

The hollyhock rust fungus (*Puccinia malvacearum*) also attacks *Lavatera* and related genera. The fungus attacks all green parts of the plant, but is most noticeable as conspicuous yellow or orange spots on the upper leaves and bracts with corresponding orange pustules on the lower surfaces. These may fuse together eventually, leading to the collapse of portions of leaves, leaving them looking unsightly and ragged. The spores are wind-dispersed and the fungus can survive during mild winters on infected leaves and plant debris. No resistant hollyhock is known but *Althea rugosa* might be less susceptible. The plants should be sprayed regularly using a fungicide labeled for rusts.

Periwinkle rust

In addition to the usual rust symptoms (*see p.41*), affected plants often fail to produce flowers, develop an erect habit, and may distort. The fungus can permeate the rootstock, so any diseased plants must be uprooted and destroyed. Since the fungus is perennial the fungicides available to control rust diseases are of limited use.

Canna viruses

Cannas can be affected by several viruses: canna yellow mottle (affects only canna), the new canna yellow streak (little is known) or bean yellow mosaic, which infects many plants, including beans, peas, freesias, and gladioli. The symptoms on canna are usually small chlorotic spots over the leaves. There are no chemical controls; destroy the affected plants.

Antirrhinum rust

The symptoms of antirrhinum rust are small, dark brown pustules on the undersides of snapdragon leaves, with a corresponding pale dimple on the upper surface. In severe attacks, leaves shrivel and die and plants are badly damaged. Spread by airborne spores, the fungus *Puccinia antirrhini* also has an overwintering spore. This rarely happens, however, and most carry-over is on plants that are kept from one season to another. Cultivars claimed to resist rust are available, but with different strains of the fungus developing, rust may still affect them. Regular sprays with a fungicide labeled to control rusts can be used. Destroy plants at the end of the season to avoid carry-over of fungal spores.

Annuals

We set great store by annuals, whether they are bedding plants from the garden center or flowers nurtured from seed. So it is infuriating if a pest or disease threatens your hopes for a garden bounty.

If you have damage on:
- Cineraria, gerbera, or oxeye daisy, see chrysanthemum leaf miner (*p.95*)

See also:
- General pests and diseases on herbaceous plants (*pp.90–91*)
- Know your enemy: pests and diseases (*pp.26–43*)

Cabbage white caterpillars on nasturtiums

Nasturtiums can be defoliated by caterpillars of the large cabbage white butterfly and, like brassicas, can also fall prey to the small cabbage white butterfly (*see p.115*) during the summer. The hairy caterpillars are up to 1½ in (40 mm) long and pale yellow with black mottling. There are two generations a year, with the hairy caterpillars appearing from spring to early fall. The best way to control them is to remove them by hand, but if they are too numerous to control in this way, spray with pyrethrum, following the label instructions carefully. If the nasturtiums are in flower, spray in the evening to avoid harming bees.

Impatiens downy mildew

The downy mildew that infects *Impatiens* (*Plasmopara obducens*) is so far confined to *Impatiens walleriana* (Busy Lizzie), but all members of the family may be at risk. The symptoms are that the leaves turn yellow and fall off the plant. It is often then reduced to bare branches and may die. Furthermore, fine white fungal growth may be visible on the lower leaf surface. To help prevent infection, space plants reasonably well apart, avoid overhead watering, and apply a general fertilizer. Affected plants should be disposed of immediately and not composted to avoid risk of further contamination. Rest affected areas from *Impatiens* for several years.

Sweet pea powdery mildew

A white powdery coating develops on leaves. It is first seen as discrete off-white patches, which may later spread on the plant. The leaves may turn yellow and die. To help prevent the problem, make sure the roots do not dry out and improve ventilation by spacing or clipping plants. You can also use fungicides approved for powdery mildew on ornamentals.

Pansy downy mildew
The symptoms of pansy downy mildew are brown-purple spots on upper leaf surfaces, usually with a surrounding yellow halo corresponding with mold on the underside. Badly affected plants shrivel and become debilitated or die. Remove affected leaves promptly and destroy infected plants if they become badly affected.

Pansy leaf spots
Two fungi cause dark and pale leaf spots on pansies, and a further fungi. causes black leaf blotches and crown rot with spores produced on the undersides of the leaves that are spread by water splash. The fungi can contaminate the soil for several years. Rotating plants and applying fungicides labeled for other diseases on ornamentals may give control.

Pansy sickness
Pansy sickness is a term loosely used to describe root and stem rot problems occurring on pansies. The foliage dies and eventually the plant is killed. Several soilborne fungi can cause these symptoms, including species of *Pythium*. Destroy infected plants. Improving drainage and applying a rotation will reduce pathogen buildup in the soil.

Nicotiana downy mildew
The symptoms of the downy mildew that affects *Nicotiana* are yellow patches on the leaves corresponding with blue mold on the undersides. The disease spreads during the season by wind-blown spores and persists in the soil as resistant spores for an unknown length of time. Destroy the infected plants and then avoid replanting.

Nicotiana viruses
Tobacco is host for many viruses, including tobacco mosaic virus and tobacco necrosis virus. Symptoms include yellow mottling, spotting, and mosaics, and can also feature distortion and stunted growth. Destroy all infected plants, as there are no cures and ensure that you wash your hands, sterilize tools, and use fresh soil.

Petunia viruses
Petunias can be affected by several viruses. Typical symptoms are yellow flecks and spots, mosaics, and streaks on the foliage. The plants may also be stunted. Destroy all affected plants immediately as there is no cure for viruses. You must always wash your hands thoroughly and sterilize tools both before and after handling petunias.

Bulbs, corms, tubers, and rhizomes

Sometimes pests and diseases of these plants are plain to see, such as insects, but if problems occur underground or during a plant's dormant phase, we may not know until it is too late.

If you have damage on:
- *Hemerocallis* and gladioli, see iris leaf spot (*opposite*)

See also:
- General pests and diseases on herbaceous plants (*pp.90–91*)
- Know your enemy: pests and diseases (*pp.26–43*)

Gladiolus thrips
These are yellowish white as immature nymphs but black when adult. They have narrow elongate bodies up to 1/12 in (2 mm) long and suck sap, causing a pale mottling of the foliage and flowers, which may fail to open. Spray with an approved pesticide when signs of damage are seen. Dispose of or burn dead tops to get rid of overwintering thrips.

Bulb scale mite
Hippeastrum and narcissus bulbs forced for early flowering indoors are susceptible to this pest. The microscopic mites live in the neck of the bulbs, where they suck sap, causing scarring along the edges of the leaves and flower stems. Growth is stunted, with leaves having a curved appearance. There is no effective treatment, so discard infested bulbs.

Lily leaf beetle
Both the adults and the grubs of the lily beetle eat the foliage of lilies and fritillaries. The adult beetle is 3/8 in (8 mm) long and bright red with black legs and head. The grubs are up to 1/2 in (10 mm) long and are reddish-brown with black heads. The grubs are often completely covered with their own wet, black excrement. Damage occurs from spring until early fall. In addition to eating the leaves of the plant, the adult beetles and the grubs also damage the flowers and seedpods. To control the pest, remove the beetles and grubs by hand, or spray the plants when damage is seen with an insecticide labeled for use against lily beetles on bulbs.

Lily disease
With lily disease, the fungus *Botrytis elliptica* causes elliptical, water-soaked spots, which appear on the leaves and may enlarge to rot the entire leaf and spread to the stem or flowers. Affected growth must be removed and burned. Good air circulation among leaves will reduce the disease's incidence. No fungicides are available to treat this disease.

Iris ink disease

The fungus *Drechslera iridis* causes black patches and streaks on the exterior of bulbs and the foliage shows yellow streaks. The leaves may turn red-brown and wither or turn black after emergence. The fungus persists on overwintered infected bulbs, crop debris, and possibly in soil. Remove affected bulbs and plant new ones in another location.

Iris rust

The fungus *Puccinia iridis* causes pale leaf spots bearing brown or black slitlike pustules and the leaves may subsequently wither and die. Older leaves are usually the most badly affected. The alternate host for the fungus is probably nettles. Cut off the worst-affected leaves and use an approved rust fungicide to help to control the disease.

Anemone smut

The cause of anemone smut is the fungus *Urocystis*. Dark streaks and blisters appear on the leaves and stems of anemones, creeping buttercups, and globeflowers. These burst to release spores, which can persist in plant debris. There are no chemical controls, but removal of the affected parts may limit spread. Rest soil from host plants for several years.

Iris sawfly

Only waterside irises, such as *Iris pseudacorus*, *I. ensata*, *I. spuria*, *I. versicolor*, and *I. laevigata*, are susceptible. Grayish-brown, caterpillar-like larvae, up to 1 in (25 mm) long, eat the foliage in summer and may cause severe defoliation. Avoid using insecticides near ponds because of the danger to fish and other pond life. Remove the sawfly larvae by hand.

Iris leaf spot

This fungal leaf spot also affects related plants such as *Hemerocallis* and gladioli. On rhizomatous irises, brown spots with yellow margins develop; bulbous irises display gray spots without a border. Leaves may die, usually after flowering. It is worst in wet years or on wet soil. Cut back diseased leaves. Fungicides labeled for use on ornamentals may help.

Mouse and squirrel damage

Squirrels and mice dig up and eat some bulbs and corms, especially crocuses and tulips. These plants are most vulnerable in the first year after planting. Firm the ground down firmly after planting to disguise the locations of new bulbs or corms. Plant in wire cages if it is practical to do so. See pages 36–37 for the limited control options.

Bulbs, corms, tubers, and rhizomes *continued*

Narcissus southern blight

This foliar disease becomes evident when the newly emerged shoots show infected tips bearing a gray mass of spores. The lesions can also be produced on one margin of the leaf. Affected leaves and flower stalks die back. Remove infected leaves, destroy bulbs on which the resting structures of the fungus (sclerotia) can be seen, and clear up leaf debris.

Narcissus stem eelworm

The microscopic nematodes live inside the bulb and foliage. Infested plants are stunted and the bulbs rot. If an infested bulb is cut transversely in half, concentric brown rings can be seen. There is no effective control. Remove infested plants and any other narcissus growing within 3 ft (1 m). Buy good-quality bulbs to avoid introducing this pest into a garden.

Narcissus bulb fly

Daffodils, snowdrops, and *Hippeastrum* bulbs are damaged by plump, creamy white maggots, up to ¾ in (18 mm) long, that eat out the center. Damaged bulbs often rot or produce just a few thin leaves. There are no effective controls. Growing the plants in shaded places reduces the number of eggs that are laid, as the adult fly prefers warm sunny places.

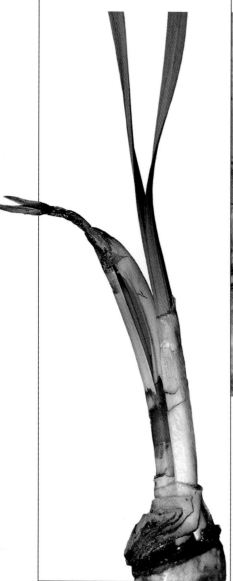

Narcissus basal rot

Basal rot is one of the most serious diseases of *Narcissus*. It is most common in hot summers when the bulbs are dying back naturally. Lifted bulbs begin to rot after a month, the basal plate becomes soft, and a red rot spreads through the inner scales, sometimes with a pink mold present. Bulbs in the soil will rot and the disease will spread to neighbors. The fungus is thought to invade through the roots, possibly via wounds, from adhering soil. Lifting bulbs in June and storing in a cool, airy place may reduce disease development. Also, it is worth inspecting bulbs and removing those that are soft. The Triandrus, Jonquil, and Tazetta groups of narcissus are resistant to basal rot disease.

Narcissus white mold

This fungal foliar disease causes elongated yellowing lesions near the tips of the leaves on which a gray white fungus can be seen. Affected leaves die back, reducing the yield of bulbs and flowers. It produces black resting structures that eventually fall in the soil. The fungus is not carried on the bulb. Maintain good hygiene and plant narcissus in a new place.

Narcissus leaf scorch

This fungal disease affects the tips of emerging leaves, which develop reddish-brown scorching that may spread down the leaves. They turn yellow and shrivel, and brown blotches may appear on the flowers. Remove the affected tissue promptly to limit the disease spread. Avoid storing the bulbs at low temperatures or planting late.

Tulip fire

Brown scorching deforms the young shoots. Sunken yellow spots with green halos appear on the leaves of neighbors. In humid conditions, the fungus shows up as a gray mold on the affected tissue. Inspect bulbs before planting for small black bodies within lesions. Destroy affected plants, as spread is rapid. Avoid growing tulips in affected soil for three years.

Snowdrop gray mold

This fungal disease is usually worst in mild winters. Growth is stunted and leaves and flower stalk rot. Diseased tissue is sometimes covered with gray, velvety fungal growth. Small black sclerotia may develop on the bulb, which rots. Dig up infected clumps and do not replant there for as long as possible. Examine bulbs before planting for the small black sclerotia.

Storage rots

Narcissus bulbs are prone to a variety of bulb rots, sometimes exacerbated by unsuitable storage conditions. Lilies and irises are prone to bulb rots where infection leads to a soft rot and a mass of blue/green spores, which usually enter through wounds. Store only perfect bulbs in a cool, shaded, well ventilated place. Avoid damaging bulbs through handling.

Dahlia smut

Circular or elliptical leaf spots arise, which enlarge, darken, and merge, but usually retain a yellow margin. The symptoms spread upward. The fungus persists as spores in the soil, but transmission does not occur in seeds or tubers. Dispose of diseased foliage in the fall and remove leaves close to the tubers before storing. Rest soil for at least five years.

Lawns

If you are looking for a perfect lawn, it is to your advantage to be knowledgeable about various pests, diseases, and cultural problems that may stand in your way. These vary from the well known—moles and fairy rings—to the more stealthy, like red thread and snow mold.

See also:
- Know your enemy: pests and diseases (*pp.26–43*)
- Beneficial nematodes (*p.63*)

Moles

Moles feed on earthworms and soil insects that enter the network of underground tunnels that each mole creates. This results in molehills where soil has been excavated onto the surface, and unevenness in the lawn surface when tunnels collapse. Mole deterrent devices are available but they are not infallible. Mole traps are more reliable (*see p.57*).

Burrowing bees

Some species of solitary bees, such as *Andrena* spp., dig their nest tunnels in short grass. They are mainly active in spring, when the female bees dig out vertical tunnels topped by a small conical pile of excavated soil. No damage is caused by this digging, and since solitary bees are useful pollinating insects, they should be tolerated rather than eliminated.

European chafer grubs

These curved beetle larvae, up to ¾ in (18 mm) long, eat grass roots. The species most frequently associated with lawn damage are European chafers. Skunks, foxes, and crows rip up the sod in fall to spring to eat the grubs. Treat with an insecticide labeled for use against chafer grubs on lawns, or apply a beneficial nematode (*see p.63*).

Leatherjackets

Leatherjackets are the larvae of crane flies. The maggots feed on grass roots and can kill patches of lawns in late winter to summer. The thick-skinned larvae are grayish brown and up to 1½ in (40 mm) long. Control larvae in early fall with a pesticide labeled for this purpose, or use a beneficial nematode as a biological control (*see p.63*).

Ants

Ants in lawns are a nuisance rather than a damaging pest. They tunnel underground and bring soil to the surface above the nest. This impedes mowing and can result in an uneven lawn surface, but little direct damage is done to the grass. Ant nests are difficult to eradicate and are best tolerated. Brush away any excavated soil to prevent mounds from forming.

Worm casts

Some species of earthworms produce a muddy excrement, known as worm casts, on the surface of lawns, mainly in fall to spring. This makes the lawn unsightly and more difficult to mow. Weed seeds are likely to germinate on worm casts. Mow grass fairly high to hide worm casts and shade out weeds. Rake worm casts when they are dry to disperse them.

Toadstools in turf

Many toadstools can appear in lawns especially following a disturbance that has increased the organic matter (fertilizing, weed-killing, scarifying). Most of these fungi (except for some types of fairy rings) are not killing the grass as they convert the organic matter into nutrients for plants. They can appear unsightly and picking them off is the only remedy.

Slime molds

These harmless organisms often appear coating blades of grass in late spring or early fall. Their color varies, but it is commonly white or yellow, and they change into gray, spherical, spore-bearing structures. They are entirely superficial and no control measures are necessary. Their appearance is short-lived, but they can be easily washed away if desired.

Red thread

Fine sod is frequently affected by this fungal disease, mainly in late summer and fall. Reddish patches of grass and pink gelatinous fungal structures appear. When dry, these can be easily spread by foot. The grass usually recovers, but improving the aeration helps, as does use of high nitrogen fertilizers and a fungicide labeled for treatment of this disease.

Fairy rings

Several fungi can disfigure lawns by forming fairy rings. The most serious form has an area of dead grass caused by the production of a dense mat of fungal growth in the soil. Spread may be halted by removing affected grass and soil to a depth of at least 12 in (30 cm), to 12 in (30 cm) beyond the edge of the ring, and replacing with fresh topsoil before reseeding.

Snow mold

Small patches of yellow, dying grass appear during moist weather in fall or spring. These turn brown and enlarge, and white or pink fungal growth may mat the grass. Improve aeration and prune overhanging shrubs. Iron sulfate can reduce the disease's severity. Do not apply nitrogenous fertilizers after summer. Also try a fungicide labeled for this disease.

The productive garden

Harvesting your own fruits and vegetables is something that is very satisfying for the gardener. However, nothing spoils this pleasure more than finding a crop of tomatoes or potatoes affected by blight, fruits damaged by maggots, and pea pods full of caterpillars. It is best to try to prevent conditions that favor problems. Identifying the cause is the first step to a cure. Once identified, treat the problem promptly before it spreads. Sometimes the damage is done before you can do anything about it, but steps can be taken to prevent pests and diseases from occurring again in the future.

Vegetables: general pests and diseases

It is a distressing sight to see a whole crop of vegetables destroyed in the garden. With good cultivation techniques and protective measures, losses can be kept to a minimum. The key is to be able to spot problems early and deal with them promptly before they become overwhelming.

The vegetable divisions in this chapter are:
- Peas and beans (*see pp.112–113*)
- Brassicas (*see pp.114–115*)
- Potatoes and parsnips (*see pp.116–117*)
- Salad crops (*see pp.118–119*)
- Assorted vegetables (*see pp.120–121*)

Cutworms These are brownish-white caterpillars of various moth species. They live in the surface layers of the soil and eat cavities in root crops and potato tubers. They also kill seedlings and lettuce by eating through the roots.

Wireworms Click beetle larvae grow into wireworms and are mainly a problem in new gardens. The slender, orange-yellow grubs are up to 1 in (25 mm) long (*see p.33*), with three pairs of short legs at the head end. They kill seedlings and bore into potato tubers, onion bulbs, and other root vegetables. Numbers decline after a year or two.

Colorado potato beetle This beetle and its reddish-brown grubs eat potato, tomato, eggplant, and pepper leaves, and may cause complete defoliation. It is resistant

There is no effective treatment for cutworms. If a plant wilts, search through the soil around the plant and remove the pest.

Wireworms bore holes in potato tubers, but there is no insecticide available for their control.

Colorado potato beetles produce chemicals that irritate eyes and sensitive skin. If hand-picking them, wash your hands afterward.

Honeybees use the holes made by bumblebees when nectar robbing to take nectar, bypassing the pollination process.

No chemicals are available to control clubroot, but various resistant brassica cultivars have been bred.

to many chemicals, so pesticides may be ineffective. Hand-pick or vacuum the adult beetles, or spray larvae with the bacteria *Bacillus thuringiensis tenebrionis* (Btt), following package directions carefully.

Nectar robbing Bees should visit the front of flowers, so they contact the pollen-bearing parts and transfer pollen to the stigma. Some bumblebees cheat and make shortcuts to the nectar in runner and broad bean flowers by biting holes in the back of the flowers. There is nothing that can be done about this.

Clubroot With this disease, plants become stunted and leaves may wilt on hot days, recovering overnight. The roots thicken and distort into a swollen mass. It can affect all crucifers and is usually introduced on seedlings brought into the garden. Improving drainage and liming the soil will help, as can raising seedlings in pots before planting them out in the garden.

White rust This disease is common on many crucifers. White chalky eruptions develop on the underside of leaves, and distortion and discoloration may correspond on the upper surface. Although unsightly, white rust is not serious and the only control measure that is required is to remove affected leaves.

To reduce the incidence of white rust, space plants well and practice crop rotation (*see p.23*).

Fruit: general pests and diseases

Garden fruit is a sweet bounty, so it comes as no surprise that it is targeted by pests. Any incidence of disease should be taken seriously so these long-lived plants do not fail.

The fruit divisions in this chapter are:
- Fruit trees: apples and pears (*see pp.122–123*)
- Fruit trees: *Prunus* (*see pp.124–125*)
- Soft fruit (*see pp.126–127*)
- Raspberries and strawberries (*see pp.128–129*)

Brown scale This is a sap-sucking insect that lives on the stems of peaches, nectarines, grape vines, plums, and cane and bush fruits, as well as many ornamental shrubs. Mature females are covered by convex, oval, dark brown shells, up to ¼ in (6 mm) long.

Winter moth The adult moths emerge in early winter and lay eggs on apple, plum, cherry, and many other deciduous trees. The pale green looper caterpillars eat the foliage and blossoms in spring before going into the soil to pupate. Prevent the wingless female moths from climbing trunks by applying sticky grease bands in the fall.

Spray a winter horticultural oil against overwintering brown scale nymphs, or spray in early summer with an approved pesticide.

To control newly hatched winter moth caterpillars, spray them at bud burst with an insecticide labeled for this purpose.

Protect fruit trees and bushes from bird damage by growing them in a fruit cage covered with wire or plastic netting (*see p.58*).

Bird damage Hungry birds can devour the unopened flower buds of fruit trees and bushes in winter. They may also eat fruit berries and peck holes in apples, plums, and pears in the summer.

Fruit tree red spider mite This is a tiny, sap-sucking pest that lives on the underside of apple and plum foliage. Its feeding causes a fine pale mottling of the upper leaf surface. Heavy infestations can develop in hot summers, resulting in early leaf fall.

Blossom wilt Many fruit trees suffer from this disease, which is worst in damp springs. Usually the flowers wilt and turn brown, and the fungus that causes blossom wilt may grow into the spur to kill leaves or form cankers on branches. Spores are blown from overwintering infections to attack the flowers as they open. Spraying at this time may reduce disease incidence.

Fireblight This is a bacterial disease that affects applelike plants in the *Rosaceae* family. It is a serious disease of pears, apples, and related ornamentals, such as *Cotoneaster*, *Pyracantha*, *Sorbus*, and hawthorn. It does not attack *Prunus* species. Leaves of affected branches wilt and brown, as if scorched by fire, and it can spread down the inner bark and result in sunken cankers.

If red spider mite is seen on apples or plums, spray the tree with horticultural oil or insecticidal soap.

To control blossom wilt, cut out any diseased tissue in summer and remove fruit suffering from brown rot.

If a fruit tree becomes diseased by fireblight, swiftly prune the affected branches and sterilize tools.

Peas and beans

Usually easy to grow, and mostly trouble-free, peas and beans are a reliable garden crop. Pea moths and aphids are the most common pests, but be prepared to deal other problems as well.

See also:
- General pests and diseases on vegetables (*pp.108–109*)
- Know your enemy: pests and diseases (*pp.26–43*)
- Potassium deficiency effects on beans (*p.15*)
- Canna viruses (*p.97*)
- Crop rotation (*p.23*)
- Barriers and repellents (*pp.58–59*)

Pea and bean weevil
The grayish-brown beetles are ⅛–¼ in (4–5 mm) long. They are active during the summer, when they eat uniformly sized U-shaped notches from the leaf margins of broad bean and peas. Leaves may be extensively nibbled, but most of the leaf survives, so the impact on established plants is small. Seedling plants may need protection by spraying with an approved insecticide.

Pea moth
Eggs are laid on pea plants in early to midsummer. The caterpillars bore into the pods and feed on the developing pea seeds. Early or late sowings of pea cultivars that flower outside the moth's flight period avoid damage. Mid-season peas can be given some protection by spraying about a week after flowering starts with a pesticide labeled for use on edible plants.

Pea thrips
Thrips have narrow elongate bodies up to 1/12 in (2 mm) long. The adults are black but the nymphs are creamy yellow. They suck sap from the foliage and pods, causing a silvery brown discoloration. Heavy attacks can occur in hot summers. Damaged pods may contain only a few seeds. If necessary, spray with an appropriate pesticide when damage is seen.

Pea powdery mildew
The discoloration on the upper leaf surfaces is caused by powdery mildew associated with a white fungal film. It is favored by dew formation. Severe infection reduces seed quality and impairs pea flavor. It survives on infected debris and may be seedborne. There are cultivars less susceptible to the disease. Early planting may help; also try sulfur to control it.

Pea downy mildew
The fungus causes lesions on the upper surface of leaves corresponding to off-white mold on the under side. Infected pods turn brown and can distort. Tendrils become bleached. Infection at emergence causes the seedlings to be stunted and to die. There is no chemical control, so remove infected plants and rest the soil from peas for several years.

Bean seed fly

The white maggots, up to ⅜ in (8 mm) long, feed on germinating seeds of runner and green beans. If the seedlings survive, they may be "blind" as a result of the shoot tips being eaten. There are no insecticides available for this pest. Seedlings can be raised under cover in pots or trays for planting out after they are past the vulnerable germination stage.

Black bean aphid

As well as broad beans, this insect attacks green and runner beans in early to midsummer. Dense colonies develop on the shoot tips and leaves, resulting in a poor crop. Pinching out the tops of broad beans once four whorls of flowers have developed makes the plants less susceptible. If necessary, spray with an insecticide labeled for this use on edible plants.

Bean rust

Dark brown pustules appear on leaves and pods of runner and green beans, and it can be more common in warm, damp summers. The white cluster-cup stage of the fungus may develop later in the season. There is no chemical control, so destroy affected tissue when seen. Avoid overfertilizing, as high nitrogen levels will increase bean susceptibility.

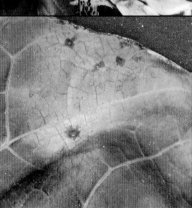

Bean chocolate spot

Chocolate spot is characterized by dark brown or gray spots on the leaves, petals, pods, and stems. Lesions can blacken, increase in size, and coalesce, leading to a destructive blight. The pathogen can overwinter in lesions. Remove infected plants. No fungicides are available. All commercial bean cultivars are at least moderately susceptible to the disease.

Bean halo blight

This is a seedborne bacterial disease where water-soaked, angular lesions appear on leaves and pods. They coalesce, becoming brown, and there is a yellow halo around spots. Red streaks appear on stems. Leaves die, stems may be girdled, and seeds rot or remain immature. Destroy infected plants, choose resistant cultivars, and avoid overhead watering.

Bean anthracnose

Bean anthracnose is caused by a fungus that causes red-brown lesions on the leaves and veins. Lesions also appear on the stems and pods. Plants collapse and seeds may shrivel. It is primarily a seedborne disease and survival on debris is limited. There is no chemical control. Use appropriate resistant cultivars as new strains of the fungus continue to appear.

Brassicas and cabbages

Plants in the cabbage family are prone to a number of pests and diseases, so learn about the problems and plan accordingly. It will be necessary to protect crops from major pests, like caterpillars or root fly.

See also:
- General pests and diseases on vegetables (*pp.108–109*)
- Know your enemy: pests and diseases (*pp.26–43*)
- Crop rotation (*p.23*)
- Barriers and repellents (*pp.58–59*)

Brassica flea beetles
All brassicas and related plants, such as turnips, rutabagas, radishes, and arugula, can be attacked by flea beetles. They are $\frac{1}{12}$–$\frac{1}{8}$ in (2–3 mm) long and mostly black, sometimes with a yellow stripe on the wing cases. They eat small holes in foliage and can kill seedlings. Encourage seedling growth by watering. If necessary, spray with an approved pesticide.

Brassica downy mildew
Yellow patches appear on the upper leaf surfaces, with white fungal growth underneath the lesions. The disease is usually most severe on seedlings. Seeds may be infected. On radishes, black lesions on the root may be seen. Improve ventilation by spacing plants. Use resistant cultivars and rotate crops, as the fungus can survive in the soil.

Brassica light leaf spot
The fungus *Cylindrosporium concentricum* causes large white blotches that contain small green flecks on very susceptible hosts, but symptoms may vary depending on weather conditions and host susceptibility. Lesions can appear on both the upper and lower surfaces of leaves. Early infection causes leaf distortion and stunting. Black spotting of the leaves and discoloration of the petioles can also occur, causing rotting of the leaves. Stems and pods can also be infected by the fungus. The disease is more severe with longer periods of leaf wetness and cool temperatures. Destroy infected plants, plant more tolerant cultivars, and practice crop rotation or leave two years between each brassica crop.

Brassica ring spot
Ring spot is caused by a fungus and is common in cool, wet areas. It causes dark spots with an angular appearance, often surrounded by a yellow halo, on leaves and pods. The entire leaf then turns yellow and, in severe infections, plants defoliate. Rotate with non-hosts, destroy all infected crop residues, and plant resistant cultivars.

Bird damage

Damage to brassicas by bird can occur at any time of year, but they are particularly troublesome in cold winters. They rip off pieces of leaf until plants are reduced to stalks. If birds prove to be a problem, protect brassicas by growing them under a cage with netting. Scaring devices, such as scarecrows or humming tapes, do not give reliable protection.

Cabbage moth

The caterpillars are yellowish-green or brown and up to 1¾ in (47 mm) long. Two or three generations occur between spring and fall. The caterpillars often bore into the heads of cabbages and soil them with their excrement. Grow under floating row cover, pick off caterpillars, or use a pesticide labeled for control of this pest on edible plants.

Cabbage root fly

The white maggots are up to ⅜ in (8 mm) long. They eat the roots of leafy brassicas, often killing young transplants. They also tunnel into the roots of turnips, rutabagas, and radishes. There are no insecticides available for this pest. Place brassica collars around the stem bases of transplants to deter egg laying, or grow plants under floating row cover.

Cabbage white butterflies

Damage is caused by the pale green velvety caterpillars of the small cabbage white and the yellow-and-black hairy caterpillars of the large cabbage white. The latter feed on the outer leaves and small white caterpillars bore into cabbage heads. Prevent butterflies from laying eggs by growing under fine mesh netting. For caterpillar control, see cabbage moth (*above*).

Cabbage whitefly

The adults are white-winged insects about 1/12 in (2 mm) in length. Both the adults and their flat, oval, scalelike nymphs suck sap from the underside of the leaves. This pest attacks all leafy brassicas. Heavy infestations soil the foliage with honeydew and sooty mold. Spray with an insecticide labeled for control of this pest on edible plants.

Mealy cabbage aphid

Dense colonies of whitish-gray aphids develop on the underside of brassica leaves during the summer. The leaves become yellowish-white above where the aphids are feeding. The growing points of young cabbages may be killed, causing "blind" plants. Grow plants under floating row cover, or spray with an insecticide labeled for control of this pest on edible plants.

Potatoes and parsnips

Parsnips and potatoes are not difficult to grow, but it can be difficult to grow them to perfection because of the pests and diseases that affect them.

If you have damage on:
- Turnips and rutabagas, see brassica flea beetles (*p.114*) and cabbage root fly (*p.115*)

See also:
- General pests and diseases on vegetables (*pp.108–109*)
- Know your enemy: pests and diseases (*pp.26–43*)
- Carrot fly (*p.121*)
- Crop rotation (*p.23*)
- Barriers and repellents (*pp.58–59*)

Potato cyst nematode
The nematodes develop inside the roots, causing the foliage to die from the bottom of the plant up. Early death of the plants results in a poor crop of small tubers. Mature nematodes appear as brown pinhead-sized objects attached to the roots. Each contains hundreds of eggs. There is no chemical treatment. Grow resistant potato cultivars on a long rotation.

Potato early blight
Dark brown spots with concentric rings surrounded by a chlorotic halo appear on the leaves, which may become necrotic and remain attached. Tuber lesions develop a dry rot. Warm wet conditions favor development. Remove debris, rotate crops, and use healthy seeds. Fertilizers and adequate water make the crop less susceptible.

Potato common scab
Scabby spots develop on the skin, with irregular edges when the skin ruptures. The tubers are unsightly, but the damage is not serious. It occurs in light soil that lacks organic matter and is worst in dry years. Dig in organic matter and water regularly when the tubers form. Do not grow on ground limed for a previous brassica crop. Resistant varieties are available.

Potato blackleg
This is a bacterial disease that can be present in seed tubers. Only one or two stems may be affected, and these blacken and rot at ground level. Remove affected plants to avoid infection of tubers, as these would not keep well. The disease is encouraged by wet soil, but potato blackleg does not persist in the soil. Buy quality seed tubers.

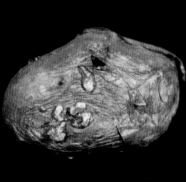

Potato dry rot
Tuber infection by dry rot *Fusarium* species only occurs through wounds. Sunken lesions with concentric rings and a white fungus can appear. Tubers become mummified. Infected seed tubers may fail to emerge or produce poor growth. Be sure they are mature when harvested and store in a cool, well ventilated place. Cultivars vary in their susceptibility.

Late blight
Dead patches at the tip of the leaflets enlarge to kill the leaf. The infection spreads rapidly under wet conditions, with spores washed to the ground to infect the tubers. The rot is a hard, reddish-brown patch. Affected tubers will not store. Airborne spores can infect plants even when no diseased material is present. Spray foliage with a fungicide before the blight appears.

Potato gangrene
This fungus causes depressions on the tuber surface. When cut across the lesion, a dark rot extends into the flesh. Black fungal structures may be in the lesion cavities and on the surface. Infected tubers are usually the source of gangrene, which invades through wounding, so try not to damage during harvesting. Destroy infected tubers.

Potato silver scurf
This is a storage disease where the fungus causes roughly circular, silver lesions on the skin that usually enlarge during storage. It does not cause yield loss but affects vigor. Transmission is through infected seeds or spores in the soil. There is no effective control, so to avoid the problem, delay harvesting, dry rapidly, and store hygienically.

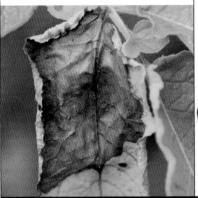 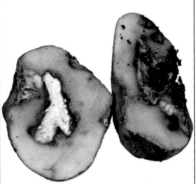 

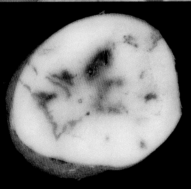 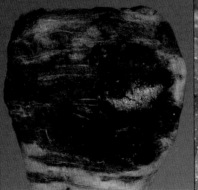 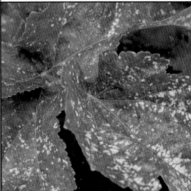

Potato spraing
Spraing symptoms are dark lines and rings on the surface and arcs, lines, or brown flecks visible in the flesh. Plants may be stunted, leaves yellowed or mottled, and tubers malformed. Destroy infected plants, plant healthy tubers, and control weeds (as they can carry viruses), rotate crops, and avoid high levels of irrigation at tuber initiation.

Parsnip canker
The fungi that cause this canker occur where lesions develop on the root. They also cause leaf spots from which spores are washed down to the soil to infect the roots through wounds. The fungi can be transmitted on or in the seed. They survive in crop debris, so remove. Rotate crops and use resistant cultivars. Earthing up may stop spores from reaching the roots.

Parsnip viruses
Yellow fleck virus causes bold yellow veins and vein netting, and then yellow flecks and mosaics. It is transmitted by several species of aphids. A helper virus is required for transmission. Weeds act as virus reservoirs as they are susceptible to both viruses. Parsnip, carrot, and celery are immune to the helper virus. Avoid susceptible hosts, control weed hosts, and spray the aphids.

Salad crops

Most salads, like lettuces, are easy to grow; others, like tomatoes, might need a bit of experience to avoid common problems.

If you have damage on:
- Radishes, see brassica flea beetles (*p.114*), brassica downy mildew (*p.114*), and cabbage root fly (*p.115*)

See also:
- General pests and diseases on vegetables (*pp.108–109*)
- Know your enemy: pests and diseases (*pp.26–43*)
- Calcium and potassium deficiency effects on tomatoes (*p.15*)
- Crop rotation (*p.23*)
- Barriers and repellents (*pp.58–59*)
- Greenhouse pests (*pp.134–139*)

Lettuce root aphid
The brownish white aphids suck sap from the roots of lettuce during the summer, causing slow growth and wilting in dry weather. They secrete a white waxy powder that coats the roots and nearby soil particles. There is no effective insecticide available for this pest. Some lettuce cultivars, are resistant to the aphid; consult your garden center or catalog.

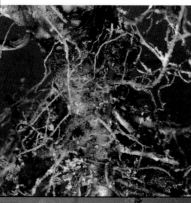

Lettuce downy mildew
Pale green or yellow areas develop on the upper surface of the leaves and eventually tissues die. Whitish mold develops beneath the affected areas. The disease spreads mainly by airborne spores, but the fungus can also survive in the soil. Dispose of affected plants, maintain a long rotation between lettuce crops, and use a fungicide labeled for use on edible plants.

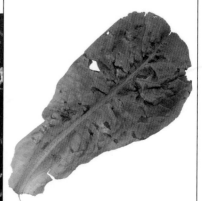

Lettuce viruses
Various viruses can affect lettuce, including beet western yellow virus, lettuce mosaic virus, lettuce big vein virus, and tomato spotted wilt virus. Symptoms of any of these viruses include vein clearing, yellowing, mosaic patterning, and deformation. Plants may be stunted. Use tolerant cultivars, remove weed hosts, and control aphids with insecticide.

Tomato fruitworm
The caterpillars of tomato moths are brown or pale green with a thin yellow line along the sides. They are up to 1½ in (40 mm) long, and between mid- and late summer they eat the foliage and fruits of tomatoes. When fully fed, the caterpillars go into the soil to pupate. Remove the caterpillars by hand or spray with a pesticide labeled for this purpose.

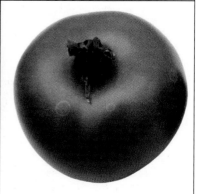

Tomato ghost spot
Ghost spot is a distinct symptom of white or yellow rings on tomatoes that occur when the fungus *Botrytis cinerea* invades the tomato fruit, but it dies prior to causing decay. The fruits develop normally and are still edible, so there is no need to dispose of them. To help remove spread of infection, reduce plant wetness and improve ventilation.

Tomato leaf mold

Patches of gray mold grow on leaf undersides and soon develop on the upper sides and turn yellow. The disease is encouraged by warm and humid conditions. The fungus survives on plant debris and greenhouse structures during winter. Good ventilation helps prevent the disease. Resistant varieties are available. Copper fungicides give incidental control.

Tomato viruses

Typically, viruses on tomatoes cause mottling and distortion of leaves, stunting, and poor fruit yield. However, it should be noted that some symptoms are very similar to those caused by herbicide exposure or cold damage. Of those that affect tomatoes, tomato mosaic virus (TMV) is a highly contagious and serious virus. Fruit can fail to set and young fruit is "bronzed" or streaked. If symptoms are seen, destroy plants immediately, although extensive spread may have occurred but not yet be obvious. Tools and hands should be cleaned well. Pest control is important. Some cultivars are marketed as resistant to TMV. Cucumber mosaic virus can also affect tomatoes (see below).

Tomato blight

Outdoor tomato plants are particularly at risk of blight, and symptoms are similar to those on potatoes (see p.117). Infected fruit discolors and rots rapidly. If fruit is picked from diseased plants, keep for five days to see if any rot develops. If nothing happens, it is safe to eat. Spray plants as soon as the first truss has set and then at ten-day intervals.

Cucumber powdery mildew

Several powdery mildew species infect cucurbits, causing early aging and reduction in yields. A white powdery growth appears on the leaves, petioles, and stems. Fruits are rarely affected. It is airborne and survives the winter on its hosts, including weeds. Improve ventilation, and use resistant cultivars. Sulfur can be used as a control on edible plants.

Cucumber mosaic virus (CMV)

This is one of the most common plant viruses, causing yellow mottling, distorted leaves, stunted growth, and a range of other symptoms on a wide range of plants. CMV is aphid- and mechanically transmitted. Destroy infected plants, practice aphid control, remove weeds, and minimize handling. Sterilize tools and wash hands. Grow resistant varieties.

Assorted vegetables

Vegetable growers need to be aware of the most common problems.

If you have damage on:

- Beets and Swiss chard, see beet leaf miner (*opposite*)
- Celeriac, see celery leaf miner and celery leaf spot (*opposite*)
- Parsley, parsnips, celery, and celeriac, see carrot fly (*opposite*)
- Radishes, see brassica flea beetles (*p.114*), brassica downy mildew (*p.114*), and cabbage root fly (*p.115*)
- Turnips and rutabagas, see brassica flea beetles (*p.114*) and cabbage root fly (*p.115*)

See also:

- General pests and diseases on vegetables (*pp.108–109*)
- Know your enemy: pests and diseases (*pp.26–43*)

Allium leaf miner

This small fly lays eggs on leeks, onions, and related plants. The white maggots feed as leaf miners and bore into leek stems. The brown pupal stage is often found beneath the base of leek leaves. No effective insecticide is available, so protect plants by growing them under floating row cover.

Leek moth

The whitish green caterpillars are up to ½ in (11 mm) long. They live as leaf miners and also tunnel into the stems and bulbs of leeks and onions. There are two generations in early and late summer. Small plants develop secondary rots and may be killed. There is no effective insecticide available. Protect plants by growing them under floating row cover.

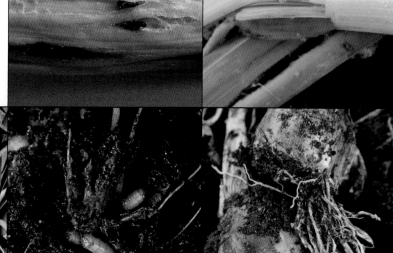

Leek white tip

The cause of white tip is the soil-borne fungus-like *Phytophthora porri*. It is specific to alliums. It causes water-soaked, elliptical blotches, mostly at tips of leaves. Badly affected leaves rot and plants may be stunted or killed. On onions and garlic, it also causes root rot. Rotate susceptible alliums with at least a three-year gap with non-host crops.

Onion fly

The white maggots are up to ³⁄₈ in (9 mm) long and there can be three generations between late spring and early fall. They eat the roots and bore into the base of onions, leeks, and allied vegetables. Young plants are often killed. There is no effective insecticide available. Plants can be protected by growing them under floating row cover.

Allium root rot

White fluffy growth appears on roots and basal tissues, which rot, sometimes causing plants to fall over. Leaves yellow and die. Destroy affected plants. The fungus produces black resting spores that can survive in the soil for 15 years, so take care not to spread contaminated soil. Grow allium species on a different site or replace affected soil.

Onion neck rot
This disease is seedborne and mainly found in storage. Softening and browning of the scales is then covered by a dense gray mold. Eventually, the bulbs suffer from dry rot and become mummified. The fungus forms sclerotia, which survive in the soil. A four-year crop rotation is recommended. Ensure that plants are dry before storing in a cool dry place.

Asparagus beetle
Both the adult beetles and their gray grubs eat the foliage and gnaw the bark off the stems. The beetles are black with yellow and red markings and are ¼ in (6–7 mm) long. The grubs are up to ⅜ in (8 mm) long. Heavily infested asparagus plants become defoliated and the stems die prematurely. Remove the pest by hand or use an approved pesticide.

Carrot fly
Carrots, parsnips, and parsley roots are tunneled by slender, pale yellow larvae that are up to ½ in (10 mm) long. Three generations can occur between early summer and fall. No effective insecticide is available, so protect plants by growing them under floating row cover. Check garden centers or catalogs for cultivars that are less susceptible.

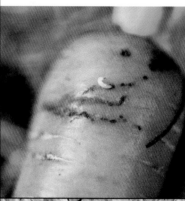

Beet leaf miner
The leaves of beets, Swiss chard, and spinach beet are mined by the maggots of this fly. The affected areas of the leaves turn white or pale green, then turn brown and dry up. Two generations occur in early and late summer. This pest is difficult to control with insecticides, so pick off infested leaves or grow the plants under floating row cover.

Celery leaf miner
Maggots of this small fly mine the leaves of celery, celeriac, and lovage, causing brown, dried-up blotches in the foliage. Two generations occur in early and late summer. Damage to young plants slows growth and makes celery stems stringy. This pest is difficult to control with insecticides, so pick off infested leaves or grow the plants under floating row cover.

Celery late blight
This seedborne disease affects celery and celeriac. Small chlorotic, angular spots that turn brown contain the black fruiting bodies of the fungus. As the disease progresses, entire leaves become blighted. Severe infections are associated with long periods of rain. Destroy infected plant debris, use disease-free seeds, rotate crops, and avoid overhead irrigation.

Fruit trees: apples and pears

Fruit trees have many pests and diseases that damage their fruits, foliage, and branches.

See also:
- General pests and diseases on fruit (*pp.110–111*) and trees, shrubs, and climbers (*pp.66–69*)
- Know your enemy: pests and diseases (*pp.26–43*)
- Crown gall (*p.68*)
- Mice and rats (*p.36*)
- Powdery mildew (*p.40*)
- Scabs (*p.41*)
- Tortrix moth (*pp.90 and 138*)
- The effects of calcium and potassium deficiencies (*p.15*)
- Traps (*pp.56–57*)
- Barriers and repellents (*pp.58–59*)

Apple sawfly
The caterpillar-like larvae feed inside apples at the fruitlet stage. Damaged fruitlets usually fall in early summer. Those that stay on the tree develop a long, broad, brownish yellow scar on the fruit skin by late summer. Remove damaged fruitlets when seen. If the tree was heavily attacked last year, spray with an approved pesticide at petal fall to control hatching larvae.

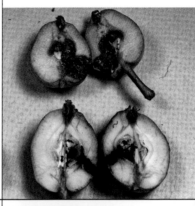

Apple capsid
This bug sucks sap from the shoot tips, causing the leaves to tear into many small holes. More noticeable, however, is the damage caused by feeding on the young fruitlets. These mature as ripe fruits that have raised corky bumps. The blemishes do not affect the eating or keeping qualities, so this is a pest that can be tolerated on backyard trees.

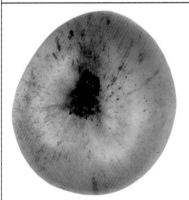

Apple codling moth
The caterpillars feed in the cores of ripening apples and sometimes pears. By the time the fruit is ready for picking, the caterpillar has usually left through an exit tunnel. Codling moth pheromone traps can be used in early summer to more accurately time spraying of recently hatched caterpillars with an approved pesticide, before they enter the fruits.

Apple leaf mining moth
The tiny caterpillars feed inside the leaves of apples and cherries, creating long, narrow, twisting white or brown lines on the upper leaf surface. Several generations occur during the summer, but heavy infestations are generally not seen before late summer. By then, it is too late for the pest to damage the tree, so control measures are not required

Rosy apple aphid
In spring, rosy apple aphids suck sap from the young foliage and developing fruitlets. This causes yellowing and curled leaves at the shoot tips. Affected fruits fail to grow to full size and have a pinched appearance at the eye end. Spray the newly hatched grayish-pink aphids with horticultural oil or appropriately labeled pesticide just before the flower buds open.

Apple and pear canker
This canker grows near buds or wounds, which become elliptical with concentric rings of shrunken bark. Spores enter through wounds. Prune out small cankered branches; on larger limbs, chisel back to green wood and treat wounds with wound paint. Spray in fall with an approved fungicide after harvest and again after half the leaves have fallen.

Pear and cherry slugworm
The larvae of this sawfly are up to ⅜ in (9 mm) long and covered in black slime. They graze away the leaf surface, creating brown dried-up areas. Pear, cherries, plums, *Sorbus*, *Chaenomeles*, and hawthorn are attacked by two or three generations between summer and fall. If they are numerous, control by spraying with a pesticide labeled for this purpose.

Pear bedstraw aphid
Dense infestations of this gray aphid can occur on pears in spring and early summer. It then migrates to plants known as bedstraws for the rest of the summer. Pear foliage becomes yellowish and distorted; it is also sticky with honeydew excreted by the aphids. Control by spraying with pyrethrin or an appropriate pesticide after flowering.

Pear midge
This gall midge lays eggs on pear flower buds. Orange-white maggots, up to ⅛ in (3 mm) long, feed inside the fruitlets. These turn black, starting at the eye end, and drop off in early summer. Destroy infested fruitlets before the maggots complete their feeding. Spray small trees with an approved pesticide at the white bud stage to control the adult flies.

European pear rust
Bright orange blotches appear on pear leaves in summer. Fruit and twigs are occasionally infected. The fungus alternates on juniper, causing perennial swelling on branches that release spores in spring. Removal of affected junipers may solve pear infection, but spores can still be blown some distance. Treating trees for scab will give incidental control.

Pear brown rot
Many fruit trees can be affected by this fungal disease. Spots of soft brown rot develop on fruit and rapidly enlarge. Rings of buff spores appear on this tissue and will initiate more infections. Rotten fruit becomes mummified and remains on the tree. The fungus can grow back into the spur. Prune out diseased spurs and remove all rotten fruit from the tree.

Fruit trees: *Prunus*

Cherries, plums, apricots, nectarines, and peaches all belong to the same group of stone fruit and suffer similar problems.

See also:
- General pests and diseases on fruit (*pp.110–111*) and trees, shrubs, and climbers (*pp.66–69*)
- Know your enemy: pests and diseases (*pp.26–43*)
- Crown gall (*p.68*)
- Hydrangea scale (*p.80*)
- Pear and cherry slugworm (*p.123*)
- Pear brown rot (*p.123*)
- Silver leaf (*see p.43*)
- Water lily aphid (*p.93*)
- Wisteria scale (*p.85*)
- Witches' broom (*p.68*)
- Traps (*pp.56–57*)
- Barriers and repellents (*pp.58–59*)

Bacterial canker
Lesions appear on branches and tissue dies above this point. Gum exudation may occur from the canker. In late fall, bacteria from the leaves are splashed onto the bark to produce new cankers. Pruning during active growth and spraying trees with Bordeaux mixture in fall helps prevent bark infection. Some plum and cherry cultivars show resistance.

Peach leaf curl
Peach leaf curl affects peaches, nectarines, and close relatives. Red or pale green blisters develop on new leaves, which swell and curl, and are later covered in white spores that may overwinter on dormant shoots. Apply a copper fungicide as buds begin to swell in late winter and again two weeks later. Spray before leaf fall and remove diseased tissue.

Black cherry aphid
Black aphids infest the shoot tips of fruiting and some ornamental cherries (not Japanese cherries). The leaves are curled and distorted, sticky with honeydew, and may turn brown. Infestations die out in midsummer. On trees small enough to spray, watch for blackfly in spring and spray with pyrethrum or horticultural oil before extensive leaf curling occurs.

Cherry leaf scorch
A leaf-killing disease of *Prunus avium* causes brown blotches to develop on the leaves during summer, which die but don't fall, even during winter. Normal growth will resume in spring. No adverse effects on the tree are seen and control is not necessary, although it may be worth removing infected leaves as they occur. Do not compost them.

Cherry leaf spot
This fungus *Blumeriella jaapii* causes round purplish spots, later turning brown on *Prunus* species. Eventually the dead tissues fall out to leave shot holes. Premature defoliation occurs and a white fungus may be seen under the leaf surfaces. Destroy infected leaves. A copper fungicide to control bacterial canker should give some incidental control.

Mealy plum aphid

Dense colonies of whitish-green aphids develop in midsummer on plum leaves and shoot tips. Large amounts of honeydew are excreted and sooty molds grow on the foliage and fruits. Spray small trees with pyrethrum or horticultural oil as soon as this pest is spotted. Sooty mold and honeydew can be wiped off fruits with a damp cloth.

Plum gall mite

Whitish-green swellings develop on the foliage of plums and damsons, especially around the margins, from late spring onward. They are induced by microscopic mites that live and feed inside the galls. Apart from creating the galls, the mites have no adverse effect on the tree or fruits, which is fortunate, as there is no effective chemical control.

Leaf-curl plum aphid

This greenfly hatches in early spring from overwintered eggs. It sucks sap from emerging leaves, causing crinkled and curled leaves on plum and damson. Infestations end in early summer but damaged foliage remains distorted. Apply a horticultural oil spray in midwinter to kill the eggs. Spray small trees at bud burst with an approved insecticide.

Plum moth

Small pink caterpillars feed inside the fruits of plums, damsons, and greengages in late summer. Damaged fruits tend to ripen early, so later-ripening fruits are less likely to be maggoty. This is difficult to control as effective insecticides are not available to gardeners. Plum moth pheromone traps can be used in early summer to capture male plum moths.

Plum sawfly

This pest has caterpillar-like larvae that bore into plums at the fruitlet stage in spring. Damaged fruitlets usually fail to develop and then drop off in early summer. There are no effective chemical controls available to gardeners for plum sawfly. In years when there has been an average to good set of fruits, the loss of some fruitlets can be tolerated.

Plum pocket

Fruits are twisted, usually one-sided, and often banana-shaped. Their skin is pale green and smooth and there is no stone. A white bloom develops over the surface and the plums shrivel. The fungus can overwinter in twigs. There is no chemical control, so remove affected plums. This disease rarely affects all the fruits and may not reappear for several years.

Soft fruit

Perishable berries like currants, gooseberries, grapes, and mulberries are dealt with here. More often than not, it is the leaves, buds, and stems that are affected.

If you have damage on:
- Gooseberries, see also currant leaf spot (*below*)
- Red currants, see also gooseberry sawflies (*opposite*)

See also:
- General pests and diseases on fruit (*pp.110–111*)
- Know your enemy: pests and diseases (*pp.26–43*)
- Coral spot (*p.67*)

Black currant gall midge
This tiny fly lays eggs on emerging leaves at the shoot tips. There are at least three generations during late spring and summer. The white maggots, up to ⅛ in (3 mm) long, prevent the normal expansion of the leaves, which remain small and distorted. There are no insecticide controls for garden use, so the leaf damage has to be tolerated.

Currant aphid
In spring or early summer, leaves at the shoot tips of red and black currants become puckered with a red or yellowish-green discoloration. Pale yellow aphids suck sap from beneath the leaves. Infestations die out in midsummer. Use horticultural oil in winter to control overwintering eggs. After bud burst, use an approved insecticide to deal with the aphids.

Currant leaf spot
A fungus causes spots or blotches on the leaves from May onward. The spots appear first on the older leaves, which may turn yellow if the spots are numerous. The disease causes the leaves to fall prematurely. Spots can occur on stems, leaf stalks, and on unripe fruits, which shrivel. Dispose of fallen material to reduce the risk of infection for the following year.

Black currant gall mite
Microscopic mites live inside black currant buds, making them abnormally swollen and rounded over the winter. Galled buds fail to develop and dry up, which reduces the plant's cropping potential. There are no chemical controls, so pick off infested buds in winter or replace heavily infested unproductive plants. Look for resistant cultivars.

Gooseberry sawflies

Several species of sawfly larvae feed on the foliage of gooseberry and red currant, sometimes causing complete defoliation. The caterpillar-like larvae are up to ¾ in (20 mm) long and pale green, often marked with black dots. Two or three generations occur between spring and the end of summer. Search for larvae and spray with an appropriate pesticide.

American gooseberry mildew

Powdery white patches develop on leaves and young shoots, causing leaves to die and shoots to be stunted. Gooseberry fruits are also badly affected. Prune infected tissue to encourage good airflow, and use a fungicide, but avoid excessive use of nitrogenous fertilizers. Keep watered and mulched in dry periods. Resistant varieties are available.

Grape erinose mite

Grape vine leaves develop a puckered appearance with a dense coating of creamy white or sometimes pink hairs underneath the raised areas. This abnormal growth is induced by microscopic gall mites. Apart from causing the leaf distortion, the mite has no harmful effect on the vine's growth or fruit. It has to be tolerated as there is no effective control.

Mulberry blight

Water-soaked spots that coalesce, turning brown and sometimes surrounded by a yellow halo, are seen on the leaves. These become distorted. Young shoots may die back and ooze bacterial slime. The bacterium can survive in leaf debris in the soil. Use healthy planting material, avoid overhead irrigation, and remove dead shoots to manage the disease.

Mulberry leaf spot

Mycosphaerella mori is a common leaf spot fungus on mulberry. It causes dark spots, which become larger and paler as the infection progresses. The spores of the fungus are water-splashed, so the infection is more commonly seen during wet summers. It can cause serious defoliation. Remove infected leaves to reduce the spread of the disease.

Red berry mite

This microscopic mite attacks blackberry fruits and interferes with the ripening process, causing fruits to remain partly or wholly red. This pest is more troublesome in hot summers. The first fruits usually ripen properly but incomplete ripening increases in the following weeks. There is no effective treatment. Use partly ripe fruit for cooking or jam-making.

Raspberries and strawberries

It makes sense to grow your own berries, given their cost at the store. Molds are a problem, but watch for other troubles.

If you have damage on:
- Blackberries, see raspberry spur blight (*below*)

See also:
- General pests and diseases on fruit (*pp.110–111*)
- Know your enemy: pests and diseases (*pp.26–43*)
- Crown gall (*p.68*)
- Barriers and repellents (*pp.58–59*)

If millipedes (*see p.34*) are a problem on strawberries, protect the fruits by lifting them up off the soil with a bed of straw.

European raspberry beetle
The slender brownish-white grubs, up to ⅜ in (8 mm) long, feed on the berries of raspberry and other cane fruits. They feed at the stalk end of the berry, causing dried-up patches. This is a difficult pest to control. Spraying with pyrethrum when the first pink fruits appear, with a second application two weeks later, will give some control.

Raspberry leaf and bud mite
The microscopic mites live on the underside of the leaves, where they suck sap. This causes pale yellow blotches on the upper leaf surface that can be mistaken for a virus infection. Mite-infested canes grow to the usual height and produce a reasonable crop of fruit, unlike virus-infected plants. There is no control for the mite.

Raspberry spur blight
Small, elliptical purple spots appear around the buds on raspberry and loganberry canes in early summer. They enlarge over the fall. The infection kills many buds, making canes unfruitful. It overwinters on canes, so remove affected tissue. Don't overfeed with nitrogen, and thin overcrowded plants. Copper oxychloride may give some protection.

Raspberry cane blight
In summer, raspberry canes may suddenly die back. At the stem base a brown lesion is present, the bark ruptures, and the stem is brittle. The causal fungus infects through wounds, so minimize damage by pruning and training. Cut back diseased wood to healthy tissue. Avoid waterlogged conditions and encourage good airflow between canes.

Raspberry powdery mildew
Several species affect raspberries. A whitish powdery coat covers foliage, canes, and fruits. Pale green blotches appear on the upper surface of leaves. Severe infection affects growth. Infected fruit may be covered with a white fungus. Severely infected berries fail to develop. Practice good hygiene and improve ventilation. Sulfur can control mildew on edible plants.

Raspberry rust
Yellow pustules appear on the upper leaf surfaces of raspberries in early summer. Later, orange then black pustules develop on the lower surfaces and defoliation may subsequently result. Destroy infected material and spray the plants with copper oxychloride before the fruits ripen. Choose less susceptible varieties for future crops.

Strawberry seed beetle
Several species of black beetles, about ⅝ in (15 mm) long, damage strawberry fruits by eating the seeds on the outside of the berry. This causes brown discoloration and may encourage rotting. Strawberry seed beetles also feed on weed seeds, so keep the strawberry bed weed-free to discourage them. There is no suitable insecticide treatment.

Strawberry green petal
Green petal is a leafhopper-borne disease. Flowers are reduced and have green petals. Cropping is poor and fruits are deformed. The plant is stunted and leaves turn red after flowering. Destroy affected plants and spray against leafhoppers. Always use certified stock when planting and replace the plants every two or three years.

Strawberry gray mold
The fungus *Botrytis cinerea* enters through the flowers and remains dormant until the fruits mature, when it can be seen as grayish growth. It spreads by contact or airborne spores and survives on plant debris or in the soil as sclerotia. Remove infected parts and plant debris. Apply a light straw covering around plants and remove weeds. Avoid overhead watering.

Strawberry leaf spot
White spots on strawberry leaves surrounded by a purple border are caused by the fungus *Mycosphaerella fragariae*. Lesions occur on flowers, fruits, and stems. Its effect on plant growth is not severe. The fungus is spread by rain splash. To control leaf spot, remove plant debris on which the fungus overwinters, and use resistant cultivars.

Strawberry viruses
Many viruses can cause decline of strawberries. Symptoms vary depending on the viruses, cultivar, and environment, but include plant stunting, yellowing, and distortion and discoloration of the leaves. Destroy infected plants and control the vector if the virus is known. Use certified virus-free stocks and resistant cultivars.

Herbs

Many herbs are trouble-free, but there are a couple of quite serious pests and diseases to consider on some of the most common plants, such as grasshoppers and mint rust.

If you have damage on:
● Marjoram and savory, see mint rust (*opposite*)

See also:
● Know your enemy: pests and diseases (*pp.26–43*)

Grasshopper on mint
Grasshoppers lay eggs in soil; they hatch in spring and eat for the entire growing season. In the garden, they prefer lettuce, carrots, onions, beans, and sweet corn; in severe years, they also defoliate trees and shrubs. Cold, wet winters and summer droughts reduce populations. Birds eat adults and robber flies, and blister beetles eat eggs. Handpick and dispose of adults.

Mint aphids
Aphids are small, pear-shaped, sap-sucking insects that eat new foliage, disfiguring and weakening mint and other herbs and vegetables. Their sticky residues attract ants and sooty mold. Hosing aphids off plants with water is an effective control. They are also preyed on by birds and beneficial insects. Insecticides are generally not recommended for use on food plants.

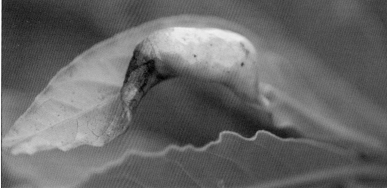

Bay sucker
The leaf margin, usually on one side of a leaf, becomes yellowish, thickened, and curled over. This is caused by bay sucker nymphs, which are sucking sap from underneath the curled leaf margin. Later, the damaged part of the leaf dries up and turns brown. Two generations of this insect occur during the summer. When the nymphs are ready to molt to the adult stage, they emerge from beneath the leaves as gray, flattened insects that secrete white waxy fibers from their bodies. Adult bay suckers may be seen on the shoot tips in summer. They resemble aphids, have wings, and are 1/12 in (2 mm) long. Pick off infested leaves as they develop, or spray with an approved pesticide when leaf curling begins.

Bay powdery mildew
Whitish patches develop on the surfaces of the leaves, which become distorted in spring and summer. Dark necrotic spots then develop, and infected leaves may fall. Increasing ventilation and making sure the roots do not get dry will help prevent the disease. Spray the plant with sulfur if the leaves are used for cooking (wait 2 weeks and wash well before use).

Mint rust

Affected stems and leaves are pale and distorted before masses of orange pustules erupt on affected areas of the stem and the lower leaf surface. These turn black as the infection develops. Leaf tissue dies and plants are defoliated. The fungus *Puccinia menthae* is perennial in garden mint and related plants, such as marjoram and savory, but spores also overwinter in the soil to infect new shoots the following spring. Use of a flame gun to remove debris in the fall and kill spores on the soil can be effective. If healthy plants cannot be obtained, heat treatment of mint rhizomes at exactly 111°F (44°C) for ten minutes before swirling them in cold water and planting is used commercially.

Lavender gray mold

Dieback of lavender can be caused by several pathogens. Some fungi enter through wounds and can be seen as black fruiting bodies (lavender shab) or gray fluffy mold (*Botrytis*) on the dead stems. *Phytophthora* causes a root rot and the plant then dies. Except for *Phytophthora* root rot, the diseases may be controlled by cutting out the infected stems.

Sage leafhopper

The mottled yellow and gray insects are up to ⅛ in (3 mm) long and readily jump off herb plants when disturbed. They suck sap and cause a coarse pale mottling of the upper leaf surface. This seems to have little impact on the plants' flavor or vigor, so the pest can be tolerated. If required, the plants could be sprayed with pyrethrum, following directions.

Cuckoo spit

Lavender is particularly attractive to sap-sucking insects called froghoppers, but they also occur on other herbs and garden flowers. The immature nymphs feed from the stems in late spring to early summer and surround themselves with a white frothy liquid called cuckoo spit. Little harm is done to the plant, so insecticide treatment is not required.

Greenhouses

The warm, protected environment of a greenhouse allows gardeners to grow tender plants. It also provides ideal conditions for certain pests to reproduce rapidly and develop damaging infestations, which, if not dealt with promptly, can overwhelm the plants. Enclosed structures, such as greenhouses and conservatories, are ideal for the use of biological controls during the summer months. Under suitable conditions, these predators and parasites are effective at keeping the main greenhouse pests at a low level without the use of pesticides. Greenhouse diseases are less troublesome, but should be watched out for nevertheless.

Pests and diseases under cover

Plants grown in greenhouses or hoop houses, or as houseplants, enjoy warm, sheltered conditions that also favor certain pests. The abundance of soft growth and high temperatures allows pests to breed rapidly. Diseases can be less troublesome under cover, but some, such as gray mold, thrive in high humidity.

Treatments and controls

Pesticides can control pests and diseases but are not suitable for all plants and have restricted uses on edible plants. Another problem is that pests that reproduce rapidly have numerous generations each year and quickly gain resistance to chemical controls. For many greenhouse pests there are alternative biological controls using natural enemies to keep pests at a low level. This avoids resistance problems and can be used on all types of plants. The predators, parasites, or beneficial nematodes are supplied by mail order biocontrol suppliers or can be ordered through some garden centers. Predators and parasites are susceptible to synthetic pesticides, so biological control is a first line of defense, rather than something to be tried after spraying has failed. Introduce natural enemies before heavy infestations have developed. They require relatively warm daytime temperatures and good light intensity, so they cannot be used in winter. If a heavy infestation is present before it is time to introduce the biological control, spray with a short-persistence organic pesticide, such as insecticidal soap or horticultural oil.

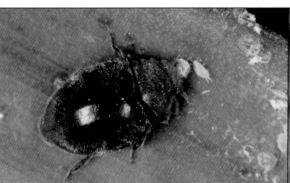

The mealybug destroyer (*Cryptolaemus montrouzieri*) and its larvae eat mealybugs and their eggs.

A predatory mite (*Phytoseiulus persimilis*) attacks a greenhouse red spider mite and its eggs.

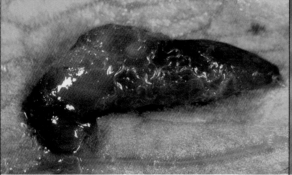

A beneficial nematode (*Phasmarhabditis hermaphrodita*) infects slugs with a fatal disease.

A parasitic wasp (*Encarsia formosa*) develops in greenhouse whitefly nymphs and kills them.

Remove dead flowers and leaves and provide space between plants to reduce fungal infections.

Integrated controls

Integrated control applies to greenhouse problems just as much as to garden pests and diseases. It involves the use of various compatible control measures instead of relying on a single control strategy, such as spraying with pesticides. This includes good cultivation practices, the use of pest- or disease-resistant plants, barriers to exclude pests, sticky traps, and encouraging natural enemies or augmenting them with purchased biological controls. Pesticides also have a role, but try to select those with a short persistence, especially if biocontrols are going to be used.

Good hygiene is important for slowing or preventing the development of diseases in greenhouses. Gray mold (see p.136) often develops on dead flowers or yellowing leaves and spreads from there to live tissues, so inspect plants regularly and pick off such material. Gray mold and other diseases, such as pelargonium rust (see p.94), thrive where plants are overcrowded and growing in humid conditions. Try to give plants space, prune out dense growth, and keep the greenhouse ventilated. Keeping the greenhouse tidy will also remove hiding places for slugs and other pests. Plants that have become badly affected by pests or diseases are best removed as they may not recover and the problem is likely to spread to other plants.

Greenhouses can get excessively hot in the summer and opening doors and ventilators may not be sufficient to keep the temperature down. Installing shade cloth or painting the glass with a shading material will help. In early fall, remove the shading as plants will need full light over the winter months.

Greenhouses need plenty of ventilation on sunny days to prevent plants from overheating.

Use a max-min thermometer to record temperatures.

Make sure plants have a regular supply of water.

Greenhouse pests and diseases

Anyone who owns a greenhouse will be familiar with the common problems, such as whitefly and gray mold, but be vigilant for other, less visible, disorders.

If you have damage on:
- Begonias, see vine weevil grub (*p.138*) and greenhouse viruses (*p.139*)
- Cyclamen, see vine weevil grub (*p.138*)
- Tomatoes, see tomato leaf mold (*p.119*) and greenhouse viruses (*p.139*)
- See also chrysanthemum leaf miner (*p.95*), and leaf and bud eelworms (*p.91*)

Red spider mite
Large numbers of barely visible yellowish-green mites live under the foliage on many greenhouse plants. They cause a fine pale mottling of the upper leaf surface, with leaves yellowing and dropping. A fine silk webbing can be seen in heavy infestations. Use a predatory mite, *Phytoseiulus*, for biocontrol, or spray with an approved pesticide.

Gray mold
Affected plant tissue rots and becomes covered in gray fluffy mold (*Botrytis cinerea*). Flowers may develop small brown spots on the petals. As it can spread very rapidly by contact between diseased and healthy tissue, ensure that dead plant material is promptly removed. This helps reduce gray mold parasitizing healthy plants. Keeping the greenhouse ventilated and watering in the morning will reduce humid conditions, which encourage the fungus. Gray mold can be a problem on grapes under glass, often infecting through the scar tissue produced by powdery mildew infection. Trying to limit powdery mildew infection should reduce the gray mold damage.

Greenhouse whitefly
The white-winged adults and their whitish-green nymphs are up to $\frac{1}{12}$ in (2 mm) long. They suck sap from the leaf undersides of tomato, cucumber, and many ornamental plants. They excrete honeydew on which sooty mold grows. Use a parasitic wasp, *Encarsia*, as a biocontrol, or spray with pyrethrum, horticultural oil, or insecticidal soap.

Fluted scale

This sap-sucking insect occurs on many plants, especially citrus plants and *Acacia* species. The mature females deposit their eggs in white waxy mounds that look grooved or fluted. Heavy infestations weaken plants and soil them with honeydew. Spray with a suitably labeled insecticide. On small plants, pick off the scales and their eggs.

Hemispherical scale

The mature females are covered by brown hemispherical shells or scales 1/12–1/8 in (2–4 mm) in diameter. They infest the leaves and stems of many ornamental plants in heated greenhouses, making them sticky with honeydew. Spray affected plants with an appropriate pesticide, or swab with rubbing alcohol. On small plants, wipe off with a damp cloth.

Oleander scale

This sap-sucking insect infests the leaves and stems of many ornamental plants in greenhouses. The mature insects are covered by flat circular scales, 1/12 in (2 mm) in diameter, that are whitish-gray with a yellowish-brown center. No honeydew is produced but heavily infested plants are weakened. Spray with insecticidal soap or horticultural oil.

Soft scale

Soft scale infests bay trees, citrus plants, *Schefflera*, *Ficus*, and many other plants. The flat, oval, yellowish-brown scales are up to 1/8 in (3 mm) long, and clustered along the larger veins on the underside of leaves. Infested plants are sticky with honeydew and often develop sooty molds. Spray with an appropriately labeled pesticide.

Tarsonemid mite

The microscopic mites suck sap from tissues inside the growing points and flower buds of many greenhouse plants. This damage stunts growth, causing scarring on the stems and leaves, and deformed spoon-shaped leaves. Flower buds often die. There is no treatment, so once the diagnosis has been confirmed, dispose of all infested plants.

Greenhouse thrips

Several species of thrips suck sap from greenhouse plants. Adult thrips are yellowish-brown or black and have narrow elongate bodies, 1/12 in (2 mm) long. The nymphs are creamy white and cause a pale mottling on the leaves and flowers. Because of their size, thrips often hide in inaccessible places on plants. Use a systemic insecticide labeled for use against these pests.

Greenhouse pests and diseases *continued*

Greenhouse leafhopper

The adults are 1/8 in (3 mm) long with mottled yellow and gray markings. The adults and the creamy white nymphs suck sap from the underside of leaves of tomato, cucumber, and many ornamental plants, causing a coarse, pale mottling of the upper leaf surface. Control by spraying with an insecticide labeled for use against leafhoppers on ornamental plants.

Mealybug

Cacti, succulents, and many other greenhouse plants are attacked by these sap-sucking insects. They infest relatively inaccessible places on their host plants and are covered with a white waxy secretion. Heavily infested plants are weakened with honeydew. Spray with an appropriately labeled insecticide, or use mealybug destroyer, *Cryptolaemus*, as a biocontrol.

Root mealybug

These white, sap-sucking insects feed on the roots of container plants. They are up to 1/12 in (2 mm) long, about half the size of mealybugs that feed on foliage. A white waxy powder coats the roots and soil particles where they are present. Treat infested plants with an insecticidal soil drench labeled for use against root mealybug on ornamental plants.

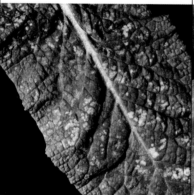

Springtails

These harmless wingless insects often occur in potting medium. They are up to 1/8 in (3 mm) long and often white. They are most frequently seen when a container plant is watered as this flushes springtails up onto the surface or out of the pot's drainage hole. They feed on decaying plant material and the associated fungal growth, so they do not damage plants.

Vine weevil grubs

Vine weevil grubs are creamy white, legless, and up to 1/2 in (10 mm) long. They eat plant roots and bore into begonia and cyclamen tubers. Most container plants are vulnerable from fall to spring. In late summer, apply an insecticidal soil drench labeled for vine weevil grubs on ornamental plants, or use a beneficial nematode, *Steinernema kraussei*, as a biocontrol.

Carnation tortrix moth

Two species, carnation tortrix and light brown apple moth, have pale green caterpillars, up to 3/4 in (18 mm) long, that attack many greenhouse and garden plants. The caterpillars bind two leaves together or fold a leaf with silk threads and graze the inner leaf surfaces. Concealed larvae are difficult to spray, so squeeze bound-up leaves to crush the caterpillars.

Fungus gnats

These grayish-black flies, ⅛ in (3–4 mm) long, run over or fly around seed trays or potted plants. The larvae are white, slender maggots with black heads, up to ¼ in (5 mm) long. They feed mainly on dead roots but can damage seedlings and soft cuttings. Control adults with sticky yellow traps. Predatory mites and a nematode are available as biocontrols.

Aphids

Most greenhouse plants attract aphids, which may be green, pink, black, or mottled. They suck sap, weakening and distorting growth. Plants are soiled with honeydew, sooty molds, and white shed skins. Apply an insecticidal spray labeled for use against aphids on ornamental plants. Predators and parasitic wasps are available as biocontrols.

Orchid viruses

Viruses are a common problem on orchids, but most of them are rare. The most important orchid viruses are cymbidium mosaic virus and odontoglossum ringspot virus. Foliar symptoms range from chlorotic streaks to black necrotic spots and line patterns. As there are no cures for viruses, destroy plants and disinfect work areas and tools.

Damping off

Seedlings collapse at soil level and roots may decay. Damping off is caused by soil- and waterborne organisms such as *Pythium*. To reduce the risk, use sterile potting mix and clean seed trays. Sow seeds thinly and use tap water. If damping off occurs, use a fungicide labeled for use against damping off on the species of seedling being raised.

Greenhouse viruses

Plants exhibit a range of symptoms when infected by viruses (*see p.41*). Under glass, three viruses are very common, and all have a wide host range. Cucumber mosaic virus (CMV) (*see p.119*) is often on begonias. Impatiens necrotic spot virus (INSV) is vectored by western flower thrips. It can affect a huge range of plants, causing diverse symptoms. Tomato spotted wilt virus (TSWV) is also vectored by western flower thrips. In dahlias it produces an oak-leaf-type ringspot pattern. Viruses cannot be cured and affected plants must be destroyed. In greenhouses where viruses are present, it is important to sterilize cutting tools when propagating. The pest population must also be controlled.

Index

Index

Acknowledgments

The publisher would like to thank the Royal Horticultural Society for their kind permission to reproduce the following photographs in this book:

(Key: a-above; b-below/bottom; c-center; l-left; r-right; t-top)

1, 5 (tr) (br). **27** (br). **29** (br). **30** (c). **31** (bl) (cr). **32** (bl). **33** (tr) (br). **38**. **39** (tr) (bl) (br). **40** (bl) (br). **41** (tr) (bl) (cl) (cr) (br). **42** (bl) (r). **43** (tr) (bl) (c) (br). **44** (l); (r).**45** (l) (c); (r). **46** (l) (c) (r). **47** (l) (c) (r). **48** (c) (r). **49** (l) (c) (r). **56** (tr) (bl). **57** (br). **59** (tr). **60** (bl) (tr). **61** (bl). **63** (br). **64-65**. **66** (tr) (bl); (br). **67** (br). **68** (tr) (bl) (br). **69** (tr) (bl). **70** (cl) (tr) (bl) (br). **71** (tl) (tc) (bl) (bc) (r). **72** (l) (tr) (bc) (br). **73** (tl) (bl) (bc) (br). **74** (tl) (tc) (bl) (bc) (r). **75** (tc) (tr) (bc) (br). **76** (tc) (tr) (bl) (bc) (br). **77** (tl) (tc) (tr) (bl) (bc); (br). **78** (tc) (bl) (bc) (br). **79** (tl) (tc) (tr) (bl). **80** (tl) (tc) (tr) (bl) (br). **81** (tc) (bl) (bc) (r). **82** (l) (tr) (br). **83** (tc) (tr) (bc) (br). **84** (tr) (bl). **85** (l) (tc) (bc) (br). **86** (tc) (bl) (bc) (br). **87** (tl) (bl) (bc) (br). **90** (tr) (b). **91** (tr) (br). **92** (tc) (tr) (bl) (bc) (br). **93** (tl) (bl) (bc) (br). **94** (tl) (tc) (tr) (bl) (bc) (br). **95** (tl) (tc) (tr) (bl). **96** (tl) (tr) (bl). **97** (tr) (bl) (br). **98** (t) (bl). **99** (tl) (tc) (bl). **100** (tc) (tr) (br). **101** (tc) (bl) (bc) (br). **102** (l) (tc) (tr); **103** (tl) (tr) (bl) (bc) (br). **104** (tr) (bl) (bc) (br). **105** (tl) (tc) (tr) (bl) (br). **108** (tl) (bl) (br). **109** (tl) (bl) (br). **110** (tl) (bl) (br). **111** (tr) (bl) (br). **112** (tc) (bl) (br). **113** (tc) (tr) (bl) (bc). **114** (tc) (br). **115** (tl) (tc) (tr) (bl) (bc) (br). **116** (tc) (tr) (bc) (br). **117** (tc) (bc). **118** (tc) (tr) (bc) (br). **119** (tl) (bc). **120** (tc) (bc). **121** (tl) (bl). **122** (tc) (tr) (bl) (bc) (br). **123** (tl) (tc) (tr) (bl) (bc) (br). **124** (tc) (tr) (bl) (bc) (br). **125** (tl) (tc) (tr) (bc) (br). **126** (tc) (r) (bl) (bc). **127** (tl) (tc) (tr) (bc) (br). **128** (tc) (tr) (bl) (bc) (br). **129** (tl) (tc) (tr). **131** (bl); (bc) (r). **136** (tr) (br). **137** (tl) (tc) (tr) (bl) (bc) (br). **138** (tl) (tc) (bl) (bc) (br). **139** (tl) (tr) (br).

The publisher also wishes to thank the following for their kind permission to reproduce their photographs:

6 Photolibrary: Rod Edwards. **8** Photolibrary: Dave Porter. **9** Alamy Images: David Robertson (t). FLPA: Gary K. Smith (c). Photolibrary: Eric Crichton (bl); Juliette Wade (br). **10** Photolibrary: Juliette Wade.

11 Alamy Images: John Glover (tr). Photolibrary: Carole Drake (cr); Andrea Jones (br). **12** Science Photo Library: Brian Gadsby. **15** FLPA: Nigel Cattlin (tl) (tc). **18** Alamy Images: Andrea Jones. **26** FLPA: S. & D. & K. Maslowski. **27** NHPA / Photoshot: Photo Researchers (bl). **28** FLPA: Minden Pictures/Silvia Reiche (br). Getty Images: Taxi/Jan Tove Johansson (bc). naturepl.com: Gary K. Smith (bl). NHPA / Photoshot: Laurie Campbell (t). **29** Corbis: Jacqui Hurst (bl). Dorling Kindersley: Kim Taylor (t). **30** The Bugwood Network: Whitney Cranshaw/ Colorado State University (r). Science Photo Library: Valerie Giles (c).**31** Alamy Images: Andrew Darrington (br). Dorling Kindersley: Emma Callery (clb). **32** Alamy Images: Bruce Coleman Inc (tl); Nigel Cattlin (br). FLPA: Richard Becker (bc); Malcolm Schuyl (tc). **33** Photolibrary: Donald Specker (bl). **34** Ardea: John Cancalosi (t). FLPA: Nigel Cattlin (bl) (br). **35** Alamy Images: Photoshot Holdings Ltd (br). **36** Corbis: FLPA/Peter Reynolds (tl); FLPA: Minden Pictures/Mark Raycroft (bl) image100 (tr); Robert Harding World Imagery/Steve & Ann Toon (br). **37** Alamy Images: botanikfoto/Steffen Hauser (br). Dorling Kindersley: Dan Bannister (t). Getty Images: DeAgostini/L. Andena (bl). **41** FLPA: Nigel Cattlin (br). **44** Dorling Kindersley: Emma Callery (bc). **52** GAP Photos: Dave Bevan (l). **53** Alamy Images: Wild Places Photography/Chris Howes (bl). Photolibrary: Michael Howes (br). **58** Dorling Kindersley: Emma Callery (br). **61** Ardea: Geoff du Feu (br). FLPA: Minden/FotoNatura (br). **62** Alamy Images: William Leaman (br). Martin B. Withers (tc). Photolibrary: Barrie Watts (tr). **63** FLPA: Nigel Cattlin (t) (bl). **72** FLPA: Nigel Cattlin (tc). **73** Photoshot: Robert Blandford/Photos Horticultural (tr). **75** Garden World Images: T. Schilling (tl). **79** FLPA: Nigel Cattlin (br). **81** Dorling Kindersley: Emma Callery (tl). **83** Kenneth Cox: (bl). FLPA: Nigel Cattlin (tl). **86** Dorling Kindersley: Emma Callery (tr). **87** Dorling Kindersley: Emma Callery (tr). **91** FLPA: Nigel Cattlin (bl). **93** FLPA: Nigel Cattlin (tr). **95** FLPA: Nigel Cattlin (br). **96** Dorling Kindersley: Emma Callery (br). **97** Dorling Kindersley: Emma Callery (tl). **98** GardenPhotos.com: Judy White (br).

99 FLPA: Nigel Cattlin (bc) (br). **101** FLPA: Nigel Cattlin (bl). photo Petr Kokeš, Czechia: (tr). **102** FLPA: Nigel Cattlin (tr). Photoshot: Photos Horticultural/Michael Warren (br). **103** FLPA: Nigel Cattlin (tr). **104** Corbis: image100 (tl). **105** FLPA: Roger Wilmshurst (bc). **112** FLPA: Nigel Cattlin (br). Garden World Images: Dave Bevan (bc). **113** FLPA: Nigel Cattlin (tl). Garden World Images: MAP/Mise au Point (br). **114** FLPA: Nigel Cattlin (tr) (bl). **117** Alamy Images: Nigel Cattlin (bl). FLPA: Nigel Cattlin (tr). GAP Photos: Dave Bevan (tl). Garden World Images: Dave Bevan (br). **118** FLPA: Nigel Cattlin (bl). **119** FLPA: Nigel Cattlin (tr) (br). **120** FLPA: Nigel Cattlin (bl). **121** FLPA: Nigel Cattlin (bl). **129** FLPA: Nigel Cattlin (bl) (bc). Science Photo Library: Dr Jeremy Burgess (br). **130** Dorling Kindersley: Emma Callery (bl). FLPA: Nigel Cattlin (tr). Michelle Ress www.flickr.com/photos/safoocat/: (tl). **134** Alamy Images: Nigel Cattlin (br). FLPA: Nigel Cattlin (tl) (bl) (tr). **135** Alamy Images: Mark Boulton (br); David Chapman (tl); Carole Hewer (bc). **136** Corbis: Tim Graham (l). **139** FLPA: Nigel Cattlin (tr) (bc)

Jacket images: Front and Back: FLPA: Nigel Cattlin GAP Photos: Maxine Adcock Zara Napier

All other images © Dorling Kindersley For further information see: **www.dkimages.com**

Dorling Kindersley would also like to thank the following:

RHS Editor: Simon Maughan
RHS Picture Research: Ian Waghorn
Index: Chris Bernstein